SUNSET STORIES
Lessons from the Dying for the Living

Paul Veliyathil

BOOKS BY PAUL VELIYATHIL

God is Plural: Sermons for an Emerging Church
Why Good News People Live Bad News Lives
T.H.R.I.V.E. Six Keys to a Fuller Life

Contact the author at
paulflorida88@gmail.com
www.paulveliyathil.com

Copyright © 2016 Paul Veliyathil
ISBN-13:978-1539490906
ISBN-10:1539490904

Printed in the United States
Createspace, Charleston, SC, 2016

Contents

Foreword

Introduction

1.	What's in a Name?	1
2.	Humanity as Divinity	3
3.	Human Being	6
4.	Career *versus* Calling	8
5.	Beyond Clinical Skills	10
6.	Are You Jewish?	13
7.	Angela's Angst	16
8.	The Beauty of Innocence	18
9.	Graceful	21
10.	Heaven's Back Door	24
11.	Heartbreaking	27
12.	History and Mystery	30
13.	Atheist	33
14.	Wiped Out	36
15.	Bad Start in Religion	39
16.	Rejection	42
17.	D.O.B. 2-13-15	45
18.	Misery Loves Company	48
19.	Vitas *versus* Vista	52
20.	Awful *versus* Awesome	54
21.	Ceramic Cup	57

22. Cosmic Container 60

23. Dead Man Driving 63

24. I Wish I could See 66

25. Death Denial 68

26. 65 is the New 45 71

27. Priscilla's Fears 74

28. Lexus and Cadillac 77

29. Dying Daily 81

30. Die Before You Die 84

31. Death is Beautiful 87

32. Endings are Beginnings 90

33. Write Your Obituary 93

34. Exit Strategy 96

35. Use the "F" Word 98

36. Procostination 101

37. Frantic Call 104

38. Death Row 108

39. Existing *versus* Living 111

40. Kevorkian Syndrome 114

41. Death with Dignity 117

42. D.N.R. Dilemma 121

43. Strangers are Family 124

44. Mondays with Morris 127

45. Can I Have Some Chips? 130

46. My Terrible Sins 133

47. I Got the Blues 135

48. Last Rites 139

49. God is with Us   141

50. A Beautiful Death   144

51. Amen   148

52. Kidnapped   151

53. Spiritual Intimacy   153

54. Eulogy Virtues   156

55. Love Handles   158

56. Facing Grief   161

57. Why Me?   164

58. Dating While Married   167

59. Finding Love Again   170

60. Skinny Little Girl   173

61. S**t Happens   176

62. Acceptance   179

63. Still with Us   183

64. Synchronicity   186

65. Bathroom Fall   189

66. Two Flat Tires   192

67. Heaven's Gate   195

68. I Could be Harry   198

69. Sol. Dad. God   201

70. Will I See Him Again?   205

71. Tired of Living, Afraid of Dying   209

72. Confirmation # MT2531-46   212

73. Tears and Laughter   215

74. Hospital Wedding   218

75. Young Old Man   222

Foreword

For most people hospice is a difficult concept to understand or talk about. The prospect of being a hospice worker is unthinkable for many because they don't want to be around dying people, and they think the work is sad and depressing. Therefore, it is heartwarming for me to see hundreds of people doing hospice work as nurses, home-health aides, social workers and chaplains at our company—VITAS Healthcare.

Paul truly enjoys his work as an inter-faith chaplain, creating a safe and non-judgmental space for people to express grief, sadness, anger, regret, tears, and gratitude. As a fellow traveler in the last stage of their journey, he reminds his patients that they are not alone. Hospice workers celebrate people's lives, reminding them of the meaning and purpose of the lives they lived, and honoring the ways they have contributed to the world.

I have had the privilege of working with Chaplain Paul as a colleague in ministry and a fellow sojourner providing spiritual care to our patients, for the past twelve years. In Florida, we are blessed with a culturally diverse, and multi-faith population. Chaplain Paul embraces the diversity and honors the human qualities that unite us as one people.

This is quite remarkable given his family history. Paul was born in India, in a country that predominately practices Hinduism, and began studying to be a Roman Catholic priest in his early teen years. After serving as a priest for 13 years, he chose a call to marriage and fatherhood and became a psychotherapist and interfaith chaplain.

He and his wife Judy have two children—Johnny and Tommy. While both sons are dearly loved, Johnny's special needs have served as a significant teacher to the Veliyathil family. Unbeknownst to Johnny, he has helped his family value the simple things in life and motivated them to look for the joy and blessings of each day.

Paul's heart is filled with gratitude and it overflows into his ministry and interactions with others. It takes a special person to want to work with patients with cognitive impairments. Paul trusts that spiritual care is indeed provided and delights in his work as a chaplain to this special patient population.

Paul believes that every life *is* a story which contains many mini-stories. During his fifteen years as a hospice chaplain, he has been a loving listener of stories of his patients who have taught him many life-transforming lessons. He has collected nuggets of wisdom from the stories of his patients and their families, and presented them in this book to educate, entertain and to inspire.

Through this book of "sacred stories," Chaplain Paul helps readers discover the sacredness and joy of hospice work, and the blessings bestowed by departing souls.

As you read *Sunset Stories,* may you recognize the spiritual dimension of people's lives regardless of their cultural backgrounds, faith traditions, social-class, level of education, or cognitive ability and may you be inspired to know that the *Holy* is within each of us and among us and continues to teach us life-lessons.

Rev. Misti M. Johnson-Arce

Chaplain, Sr. ACPE Supervisor

VITAS Healthcare, Broward & Palm Beach Programs

Introduction

"It takes a special person to do what you do." As a hospice chaplain, I have heard that phrase too many times. I don't take that compliment as an ego-boosting supplement. I believe that every person is special, and every job can be special if done with mindfulness and joy.

Being surrounded by death on a daily basis is hard, being with the grieving is exhausting, and comforting the bereaved can be challenging, but the payoff is huge.

Every person *is* a story that contains many mini stories. All you need is a kernel of curiosity, an ounce of warmth and a willingness to listen. Listening to stories of my hospice patients for fifteen years has transformed my life.

I believe that being part of the life-journeys of individuals, days or weeks before their death, is a privilege. It is an honor to be invited into the inner sanctums of their lives; it is humbling to listen to their stories; it is heart-warming to hold their hands and say a prayer. I am amazed by their grit, amused by their wit, and attracted to their amiable traits. When you are at the bedside of a person who is in her 90's, you are witnessing history, touching mystery, and beholding a miracle.

Every human interaction has the potential for *information, inspiration,* and *transformation.* How those possibilities play out largely depends on your *disposition.* For example, if you walk around a shopping mall daydreaming, you are unlikely to be impacted by the passers-by, and the happenings around you. Or if you talk on the phone at the checkout counter, and pay no attention to the clerk in front of you, you will miss a great opportunity to make an impact on that person and receive grace in return. Similarly, if I visit a hospice patient, just as a patient and not as a person, I miss out on a lot.

It is a given in sociology that our interactions come with a set of biases and prejudices that we have acquired on the way to our human maturation. They can be good or bad, but they exist. We see the world as *we are,* not as it is.

Ever since I realized that the word *listen,* is anagram of *silent*, the way I listen to people changed. It is a fact that most of the time when we listen to others our mind is distracted or pre-occupied. We listen with the intention to counter an argument or to interject our own story, instead of hearing out the story of the person talking to us. I have learned that unless I become *silent* within, I cannot *listen* effectively.

Psychologists have suggested several techniques to help in our interactions, such as suspending our biases, asking open-ended questions, being respectful, apologizing in advance, etc. They are all useful and effective, to a point.

I use a different method: to approach every human interaction with a sense of *curiosity, generosity,* and *unity.*

This approach has helped me with an amazing fifteen years as a hospice chaplain during which I never worked a day, but had the best job in the world.

Curiosity means not taking people for granted. Every human being is a mystery to be unraveled, and has a history to be explored. When I sit in front of my patients who are in their 80s and 90's, and a centenarian every now and then, I am sitting in front of living monuments of unfathomable mystery and tangled history. I am curious about their lives during their various stages—a child, a student, a young person falling in love, couples getting married, parents raising children, their jobs, travels, accomplishments and disappointments, ideas that triggered their imagination, projects that propelled their position in lives, challenges faced, tragedies suffered, and dreams differed—there is so much to learn from them, and yet at the end of all that learning, I am still left with mystery.

Generosity in interactions involves withholding judgments and refusing to label and categorize people. I make a conscious effort not to put on labels such as *difficult, weird, nasty, crazy, odd,* etc. on people with whom I interact. Trying to categorize ninety years of life of an individual under a single label is both unjust and unkind. Generosity of spirit for the perceived flaws and foibles of others always opens doors to the interior castles of their hearts.

Unity is about seeing the *connection* between individuals despite the apparent sense of *separation* between them. I believe that strangers are family I haven't met *yet*. Once I meet them, the label *stranger* is replaced by *sibling*. By consciously affirming to myself that s*eparation* between humans is an *illusion,* I have been able to see others as an extension of myself with feelings, hopes, and dreams similar to mine. This awareness has helped me to genuinely love my patients, and approach them with awe, and learn from them life-changing lessons.

There are 75 stories in this book. For most stories, names have been changed to protect the identity of the individuals; but for some, actual names are used because the protagonists wanted their stories to be told.

I thank my fellow chaplains Kevin McGee, Larry Schuval, Steven Jugens-Ling, Grellet Sainvilus, music therapist Tom Dalton, and my friends Jack Bloomfield and Bill Kieffer (hospice volunteers) who have contributed their stories.

The stories in this book are about the valuable life-lessons my patients have taught me. They have influenced my thinking, impacted my being, and shaped my life. I offer them to you with the hope that they will make you laugh and cry, wink and wince, celebrate the human spirit, and help you make your life-journey an enjoyable ride.

Approach these stories as *protagonist* and *ponderer*. The *Ponder and Practice* section at the end of each story is offered as a guide to that process. However, feel free to ask your own questions and wrestle with the feelings the stories may evoke in you. You are likely to benefit more if you read them slowly, and in small increments rather than read through the book.

Let the stories challenge your assumptions, examine your biases, and help you embrace your vulnerabilities. Let them expand the boundaries of your imagination, and stretch the edges of your faith. May they widen the horizons of your curiosity, and take you to a state of flourish and flow.

1. What's in a Name?

I was born and raised in Kerala, India. I have lived in the United States for twenty eight years. During these years, only very few people have attempted to pronounce my last name and only a handful have succeeded. Most people either mangle it or give up and say, "I'll just call you Paul." During those moments, I had fleeting thoughts about changing my name to *Paul Smith.*

About twelve years ago, I googled my name and there were 178 results. Today there are 2080 results on Google. But the surprising revelation is that I am the only *Paul Veliyathil* on the planet, at least according to Google. The same is true of the white pages of the phone book of my city.

On the other hand, the name *Paul Smith* has more than 776 million results on Google. That day, I decided, once and for all, that regardless of how many people mispronounced my name or considered me a *foreigner,* I was going to keep my name and be proud of it. Besides, my chance of being a victim of identity theft is less as most criminals won't bother to fabricate a unique name such as mine.

Once, I experienced the greatest blessing of my name when one of my patients tried to pronounce it. Dolores was 79 years old, with a diagnosis of Alzheimer's disease. She was charmingly confused, blissfully ignorant, and a joy to be around because she was so innocent and playful. She reveled in the attention I gave her, and I enjoyed the experience of looking into her twinkling eyes and wondering what an amazing life she has had before Alzheimer's set in. Every time I am in the presence of patients like Dolores, I am elevated to the realm of mystery and wonder.

Dolores tells me that she is 30 years old and her husband is 25 and that they have a 35 year-old daughter. When I point out that is impossible, she squeezes my hand and laughs with a mischievous twinkle in her eyes. Regardless of the content of our mundane and disjointed "conversations," I always enjoyed visiting her, because there was a pure joy that comes from being in the presence of someone going through a "second childhood."Anyone who enjoys being with little children will enjoy being with Alzheimer patients, because they are like children in all aspects, except in size.

During a visit, Dolores asked me what my name was, and I said "Paul." I did not want to confuse her with a name that many so-called "normal people" find so hard to pronounce. She insisted on knowing my last name, so I showed her my VITAS badge. She looked at it intensely for a few seconds, looked into my eyes, and asked, *Veryfaithful*?

My jaw dropped and tears welled up in my eyes. I was instantly elevated to a place of gratitude and grace. I felt as if Dolores had peered into my soul and invited me to live up to the meaning of my name as she saw it. I took it as an affirmation of my life and as a challenge to be faithful to God, faithful to other human beings on this planet, and faithful to life itself.

* * *

Ponder and Practice

> Do you like your name? Does your name have a meaning? How do you live that meaning?

> We all love the sound of our names. Learn names of people you interact with and use them during conversations.

> Name one person who has influenced and inspired your life the most. Offer a "gratitude prayer" for that person.

2. Humanity *as* Divinity

March 18, 2006, was my first day of work at the Broward Program of Vitas Hospice. I was hired as the new chaplain for Team 145, a group of 17 individuals—a doctor, a social worker, six nurses, seven CNAs, team secretary, and the team manager. I had not met anyone on the team except the manager. So, I was little nervous waiting outside the meeting room, and the first person to greet me was Susan. Seeing me standing there alone and vulnerable, she approached me and asked: "Are you the new guy, I mean chaplain, who is joining our team?" I said yes, and we shook hands.

There was this knowing smile on Susan's face, and I said to myself: "This is a safe place."

I have identified three kinds of smiles during the initial meeting between individuals. The first is called "nervous smile," an awkward smile due to unfamiliarity with the person. The second is called "cautious smile," because the person is a stranger. The third is called *"déjà vu* smile"—I *know* this person and I like him. I had never met Susan before, but at that moment, I felt as if I had known her for a long time. Our continued interactions and friendship for the next two and a half years proved just that.

The following day, I was sent to an assisted living facility where Susan worked, to "shadow" her and get familiarized with the facility and the patients. While she was taking me around, one of the residents approached her and asked: "Who is this young man with you today?"

Susan put her arm around me and said: "Oh, this is my new husband, Paul." I enjoyed the pure innocence of that moment. I loved the openness and freedom of this woman whom I had met just 24 hours earlier.

Susan had a transparent quality to her personality. She had an uncanny ability to instantly connect with people through her beautiful smile, humorous words, and ability to meet at the level of sheer humanity. She did not pretend or wear any facade.

A year after I began working with her, Susan was diagnosed with ovarian cancer. It was a difficult journey for her, but she endured the anxiety of the diagnosis, the agony of the chemo treatments, and the last days on hospice care with a sense of dignified calm rarely seen in such situations.

My relationship with Susan was ironic because she disagreed with everything I believed regarding God and religion. She told me straight out that she was an atheist. She thought that religion was man-made, that God did not exist, or had He existed, He didn't care. When I talked about religious topics during team meetings, Susan would roll her eyes. When the team manager told her that she prayed for her every morning, Susan said that was just "crap."

Every time I hugged her, I would whisper in her ears, "God bless you and I love you." And she would say: "I understand the "I love you" part, but God blessing me? That is baloney." "If God is so great, why is He *blessing* me with this cancer?" she asked.

Susan and I had many discussions about God, religion, and prayer. What Susan rejected was belief in a "theistic" God, an old man with a white beard separated from humans; someone who hears some prayers and ignores others, who blesses the chosen and punishes the wicked. I don't believe in such a God either. When I talked to her about God as the "Universe" and prayer as "energy" she seemed to be open.

Susan did not assent to a set of beliefs, recite any creeds, or attend any temple, but she manifested "godly" qualities in her behavior. She may not have believed in the Holy Spirit, but she demonstrated what Christians call the "Fruit of the Spirit" in her life—love, peace, joy, patience, kindness and goodness.

One day when I visited her in the hospice unit, there was another visitor in the room. This is how she introduced us to each other: "Paul, this is Tony who I drink with, and Tony, this is Paul who I pray with." And then she rolled her eyes.

Two weeks before her death, she asked me for a favor: "Paul, would you speak at my funeral?" It was an honor and a blessing bestowed upon me and I kept that promise.

For two and a half years, I sat next to Susan during team meetings. When certain things happened in the meeting, Susan would poke me on the side or roll her eyes and I knew exactly what she meant.

This Catholic priest from India who is obviously religious, and a Jewish woman from New York who was anti-religion, connected beyond religion, beyond nationality, beyond color, and beyond man- made labels. We connected at the level of our common humanity.

I believe that humanity, at its best, is divinity!

* * *

Ponder and Practice

> Is it possible that the "Holy Book" can be an obstacle to what the "Book" demands, i.e., loving others?

> What is your initial feeling when you meet somebody for the first time? Is it caution, suspicion or affection? Explore the origins of those feelings.

> Say a prayer in the morning for the generosity of heart to look at every person you meet that day with affectionate eyes.

3. Human Being

I am a member of a diverse group of about thirty five hospice chaplains belonging to several religions, such as Buddhism, Judaism, and Christianity with its various denominations. During our monthly meetings, self-introduction will be on the agenda if there is a new chaplain joining the group. In the interest of time, we introduce ourselves by name and denomination only.

So we started from one end: *"I am Joe, and I am a Presbyterian," "I am James, and I am Baptist;" "I am Mark, and I am Southern Baptist;" "I am Patrick, and I belong to Church of Christ,"* and the next one said, *"I am Janice, and I belong to the United Church of Christ,"* then the next one, *"I am Nick, and I am Methodist,"* and the next one, *"I am Cathy, and I belong to the United Methodist Church."* And it went on until 35 of us introduced ourselves as representing a specific religious denomination.

When my turn came I said: *My name is Paul and I am a human being.*

Everyone chuckled and the meeting continued. During the break, the Rabbi who was new to the group that day, took me aside and said that she was intrigued by my introduction and wanted to talk more about it. I told her that I was not trying to be a wise guy or being flippant about it. According to the *World Christian Encyclopedia* (Second edition 2001), global Christianity has 33,820 denominations which I believe is an abomination and an affront to Jesus whose final prayer was for unity among his followers. By 2025, the number of Christian denominations is expected to exceed 55,000!

God did not create any denominations. Humans created them mostly for selfish reasons.

I told the Rabbi that if I say I am a "Catholic," which I am by baptism, I am connected to about 1.5 billion people because that is the total number of Catholics in the world. If I say I am an "American," which I am by citizenship, my connection shrinks to 320 million people. If I say I am "Indian," which I am by birth, I am connected to 1.2 billion people.

These three identifications connect me to about 3 billion people, but I will still be unconnected to about 4.2 billion people out there, because there are more than 7 billion people on this planet. "Human" is the only title that connects me to everyone. Human being is the only label that brings me into communion with the whole world.

Apostle John said, "God so loved the world that he gave his only son." Christians usually focus on the second part of that sentence about the "only son" and forget the first part, "the world." It does not say, God so loved America or God so loved India or any particular nation or any specific group of people, but God loved the "world."

When you expand your mind to embrace the world, and all the people in it, you are manifesting your godliness and in that process, experiencing God.

* * *

Ponder and Practice

> Make a list of the labels placed on you by society, culture and religion.

> Are you aware of the origin and meaning of those labels or are you wearing them without thinking about them?

> Imagine living in a world where everyone has the same label: *human*. In fact, that is a *fact*. Peel of some fake labels and see how that feels!

7

4. Career *versus* Calling

About 3500 times a day, Laura answers the phone saying: *Vitas Health Care, how may I direct your call?* One day, while stopping by her desk, I asked: "Do you ever get tired of repeating the same phrase thousands of times a day? "No, this is my job," she replied.

Laura is not merely a switchboard operator behind closed doors somewhere at the back of the building. She is also the receptionist, the first person visitors see as they walk into the Broward County office of *Vitas Health Care*. She directs both telephone traffic and foot traffic into the office building of our hospice program. She greets everyone with her characteristic gentle smile. It is a hectic job that requires calm presence and it is so easy to get frazzled and frustrated on that job. Laura handles it gracefully.

I had always wondered how she managed such a high pressure job with such ease and grace. But there is never enough time to ask that question and get an answer because during a one minute conversation, she could be interrupted twenty times—literally—that is about 20 calls a minute, sometimes more.

My work is mostly in the field visiting patients in assisted living facilities. I go to the office only once a week for team meetings. Those days, I make it a point to visit with Laura for a few seconds, because as President George H.W. Bush once said, Laura is one of those "thousand points of light." I stop by at her desk to re-ignite my spirit and to fan the faltering flame of my soul-candle and I am never disappointed.

During my last stop, she asked me: "Would you like a piece of bread?" It was an unusual question from a very busy receptionist; besides I didn't spot any bread on her desk. I was intrigued and interested. She pointed to a little box on the side of her desk containing a stack of colored strips. I picked one and it read:

My grace is sufficient for you (2Cor: 12:9). My eyes welled up with tears. I needed that message that day to ground myself and feel fully confident in the protective arms of God.

Laura told me the story of a visitor to the office who had ovarian cancer. This visitor was obviously having a very hard time with that fatal diagnosis. Laura gave her a "piece of bread." She took and read it. It happened to be from the gospel of John: "Let not your hearts be troubled, trust in me and trust in my Father." The visitor left, but few months later she came back to thank Laura and to report that her cancer was in remission.

Laura is an amazing apostle of peace and grace. She is doing a very important job for the company, and she has turned that hum drum job into a ministry. Laura is a great example of how our attitude can make a huge difference in the world. She is a living proof that what matters is not what we do in our job, but what we do it with—our approach and attitude.

Laura is a living testament to the truth that the most insignificant and boring work can be turned into an opportunity for making a difference in the lives of others. Thank you Laura, for your inspiring witness.

* * *

Ponder and Practice

> If your Job feels like a Chore that is Aggravating, Rough, Exhausting, Empty, and Robotic, more than likely you are in a CAREER. On the other hand, if you see it as Challenging, Affirming, Loving, Lively, Interesting, Nice, and Gratifying, you have a CALLING.

> Take a few minutes to evaluate your current job and make a list of things you like about it and dislike about it.

> Think about five things you can do now to change your job from a mere CAREER to an exciting CALLING.

5. Beyond Clinical Skills

James was a chaplain intern who was assigned to me to show him the ways and waves of hospice chaplaincy. He was slightly shy but very polite, professional, enthusiastic, eager to learn, focused, dedicated, compliant and committed.

After observing me for three days of visiting patients, James took the lead in visiting a patient while I took the role of observer.

The patient was a 98 year old Jewish male named Joseph, diagnosed with heart disease. He was fully oriented and capable of real time conversations. He was pleasant, friendly, and welcoming of the visit. Joseph had a great sense of humor, and laughed out loud several times during the visit for no apparent reason.

Since the patient was slightly hard of hearing, and James was a fast talker, many questions had to be repeated. There were moments of awkward silence where James got stuck, not knowing what to say or how to respond.

To break the silence, James asked: "So, how are you doing otherwise?" which is a more appropriate question for a friendly conversation than a clinical dialogue. And he continued:

"So, what do you think of God?," which I thought was a loaded question appropriate for a theology 101 class, not a question for a 98 year old hospice patient. Joseph glossed over that with no response.

Joseph: "I had a miserable childhood." (No follow up from James; a moment of silence)

James: "Are you ready to meet God?"

Joseph: "I am an old man."

James: "I know..." (!!!)

Joseph: "You are not Jewish, are you?"

James: "No, I am not." (Sounded a bit defensive)

At the end of the session, I told Joseph that James was in training to be a chaplain. Joseph had forgotten that, even though James was introduced as such at the start of the visit.

Joseph's response was very revealing of what hospice chaplaincy, and in fact, what life is all about. He said to James: "You did great; on a scale of 1 to 10, 1 being the worst and 10 being the best, I will give you a 12!"

From a clinical point of view, the interview was imperfect at best. But the patient's response indicated that, from a spiritual point of view, it was more than perfect.

I was once again confirmed in my conviction that the best tool we have in our armory as chaplains and humans is ourselves— the demeanor we project, the energy we emanate, the compassion we communicate, the ease we create, and the unconditional positive regard that envelopes our environment. I believe, that as a spiritual being, *I am the sacrament* that soothes pain, eases tension, harnesses hope, and brings healing and comfort to the patient.

James was such a personal sacrament to Joseph that Friday.

Joseph's response reminded me of Maya Angelou's powerful words: "Years later people will forget what you said to them or what you did for them, *but they will never forget how you made them feel.*"

We affect others more profoundly through our *being* rather than our *doing*.

James's words may have been inappropriate, and his communication skills may have needed tweaking, but he had a gift that is greatly needed, and matters most in this line of work— personal grace.

* * *

Ponder and Practice

> Think of those individuals who have influenced your life. Are you impressed by their performance (doing), or by their personality (being)?

> Where do you see your strength—in your being or in your doing? What is the percentage of your personality *versus* performance scale?

> Make a list of ten words that people who know you would use to describe you. Remember that you are a moving "container of energy" and that you always leave behind—a stench or a scent!

6. Are You Jewish?

More than forty percent of patients on my hospice team are Jewish. While most of them are open to a visit from a chaplain, some are reluctant. I always call the caregiver, to ask permission to visit the patient. In this case, it was his daughter. She told me that her father was 88 years old, and has been an orthodox Jew all his life. "He is unlikely to be receptive, but you are welcome to try," she said.

Since Marvin lived in an assisted living facility, an appointment was not necessary. I went with the hope of visiting with him, but if he refused and requested me to leave, no big deal. I can always visit another patient in the same facility.

The staff at the facility told me that Marvin was a little bit on the "grumpy" side and that he has his good days and bad days. They warned me that he could be rude, and that I should not take it personally.

There was a time in my life I took every little reaction from others personally, but not anymore. I have come to the awareness that everyone does his or her best in any given circumstance and that 99 percent of the time a person's reaction to me has everything to do with him/her rather than me. This approach has helped me raise the level of my "offense meter" to new heights.

I said a prayer in my heart for Marvin and for myself, and then gently approached his room which was wide open. He was resting in his reclining chair. Entering the room I said: "Good morning, Mr. Marvin, how are you today?"

No response from Marvin except for a suspicious look. "Suspicious" in my judgment, but he was just being himself. Again, I am cutting and pasting my perceptions onto the manners and motives of others.

"My name is Chaplain Paul and I came to see you," I said. Marvin responded with a question: "Are you Jewish?" I was taken aback a little, but with an inspiration that came to me out of the blue (aka, God), I said: "I am the last Jew out of India." Marvin laughed out loud and asked me to sit next to him.

During the next 90 minutes we talked about everything—his life, family, two daughters, four grandchildren, his business in New York, his wife, the many cruises they took together, his temple. We got along fine, and I visited him many more times until his death eight months later.

Humor is definitely a great tool to break barriers and engage people. As Danish Comedian Victor Borge once said, "laughter is the shortest distance between two people." But more than humor, what helped me that day was my desire to see people beyond their labels. I did not look at Marvin as an orthodox Jew who needs to be "saved," but as a human being to be engaged, and that way of "seeing" somehow helped Marvin to open up. I was more interested in our common humanity rather than in our differing religiosity.

I grew up in a Catholic home and became a Catholic priest. Until 1962, the Catholic Church officially taught that there was no salvation outside the Church. Yes, it meant outside the "Catholic Church," which excluded even the millions of Protestants! Forget about the Hindus and Chinese...they have no hope!

I never believed in non-salvation for the "non-Christians." In fact, I stopped using the word "non-Christian" as a designation for adherents of other religions. I call them by their names: "Hindus," "Muslims," "Jews." Why should they be defined in reference to my religion? When I call adherents of other religions "non-Christians," I am defining them negatively. I am being the "norm" and they are being the exception.

No one is an exception. There is no "chosen people." God is not a partisan. Everyone is included in the wide tent of God's love and grace. When I approach patients with unconditional positive regard, every encounter is eased with peace and grace.

* * *

Ponder and Practice

> What is your religious affiliation? Were you born into that religion or did you choose it? What is the difference?

> Write down five intelligent statements each about Hinduism, Islam, and Buddhism, excluding statements like "Hindus worship cows," "Muslims are terrorists," and "Buddhists meditate."

> Visit a place of worship other than yours. For example, if you are a Christian, visit a Hindu temple, a Synagogue, and a Mosque during their worship hours. Write down your feelings before and after the visit and compare them, and possibly discuss with a friend or colleague.

7. Angela's Angst

I had a patient named Angela who lived alone in her apartment. She was 90 years old but was able to manage herself with limited supervision from her daughter who lived nearby. I was her only constant visitor. Every Friday, she would wait near the window, looking through the blinds for my arrival.

One Friday, I found her extremely upset and distressed because her TV had stopped working. Television was Angela's life-line. She always kept it *on* to mask the monotony of loneliness. Without her TV, she felt afraid and lonely.

Angela was on a limited budget and the thought of paying for a repair man distressed her. When I walked in, she began crying. She told me that her TV had stopped working and asked me if I could repair it. Being totally mechanically challenged, I didn't dare. When Angela went to the kitchen to make a cup of coffee, I just looked around, and to my surprise, I found out that the TV was not fully plugged into the outlet. There was a table lamp next to the TV, sharing the same outlet, and it had come lose, but Angela did not have the ability to check behind the giant TV. I plugged it in, and voila, *The Price is Right* came on! "Angela, it is a miracle," I cried out in excitement.

She could not believe her eyes. She hugged me tightly and said: "You made my day; you have no idea what this means to me. I thank God for sending you here."

That day, I realized that a simple act like plugging in a TV can make a huge difference in someone's life, and that apparently insignificant and unimportant things can be significant and meaningful for others. I also determined never to judge the impact of my behavior on others based on my perceptions, because what I consider to be insignificant could be very significant for somebody else.

The thought of "Almighty God" being concerned about an

old lady's television and "sending" me to her may be considered "faith-stretching." But maybe not! The God, who adorns the fragile lilies of the field and takes care of the tiny sparrows of the air, is equally, if not more, concerned about Angela's TV too.

There is a saying that "when a butterfly flaps its wings in San Francisco, weather changes in Singapore." It is a poetic way of saying that every little act can make a difference in somebody's life, somewhere in the world, like the ripple effect of a small stone thrown in the middle of a lake causing waves all around.

My prayer today is that the Jesus, who takes note of the *widow's mite,* (Mark 12: 43) impress upon me once and for all that everything I do is important in the eyes of God, so that I may do it with compassion and devotion; that I won't look at anything casually, or treat anyone callously; and that I will pay attention to every event, relish every experience, embrace every moment, and cherish the person right in front of me.

* * *

Ponder and Practice

> Make a list of ten people in whose life you are making a difference today.

> If you were to die today, who will be most affected? How and why? Write down in detail all the ways they will miss you.

> Make it a daily practice to offer at least three compliments to the people around you.

8. The Beauty of Innocence

The patients served by my hospice team are residents of assisted living facilities, ranging in ages between 80 and 100. Most of these facilities have separate units for Alzheimer's patients. There is a sadness that follows me into those locked areas of human beings who are unaware of their identity, their location or even the time of day, day of the month or the year. There is also a joy that arises in me as I abide with them for a few hours.

These are accomplished individuals who are confined to wheelchairs, and they depend on others for their survival and well-being. They are unable to express their needs or engage in meaningful dialogue.

There are some who can "talk" non-stop, using a string of words with no specific meaning. I find great joy in being with them and engaging them in "conversations."

Millie is 89 years old. She owned a clothing store in Queens with her husband and they raised five children. She enjoys the love and attention I give her. She can talk non-stop and often it is a disjointed dialogue. Here is a sample of our "conversation."

Me: "How are you today, Millie?"

Millie: "Who are you?"

Me: "This is Chaplain Paul, remember?"

Millie: "*Captain* Paul?"

Me: "No, *Chaplain* Paul. The guy from India."

Millie: "Oh, from Indiana?"

Me: "No, from India…you look beautiful today."

Millie: "I am a nice Jewish girl."

Me: "Yes you are; had I met you years ago, I would have asked you for a date."

Millie: "My husband would beat you up."

Me: "Where is your husband?"

Millie: "He is in the other room."(She has been a widow for a decade)

Me: "I am happy to come and see you today."

Millie: "You have an oval face, your nose is turned up, your ears are big, and I don't know why."

Me: "I don't know either."

Millie: "You are the most pleasant person I have met in a long time."

Me: "Thank you."

Millie: "But you are not perfect; I like tall people and you are not tall, but you are OK."

Me: "Thank you Millie for the compliment."

Millie: "You are a nice looking man and that helps."

Millie is like a child, and she speaks without filters. In her disconnected words and disjointed phrases, there is a beauty and innocence that is inherently graceful.

At the end of the visit, she squeezes my hand, and I tell her again that she is a beautiful person. Millie laughs and says: "I am an old lady."

If "laughter is the sun that drives winter from the human face," the winter of dementia and loneliness has been lifted for Millie, at least for an hour.

* * *

Ponder and Practice

> List the names of your grandparents. Is there something that they said or a lesson they taught you that continues to have an influence in your life today?

> The elderly usually speak without filters. Knowing not to take them literally or personally will help you deal with them with understanding and compassion.

> *Pastoral Presence* is a phrase associated with chaplaincy and ministry which emphasizes the power of your "presence." Pastoral presence is much more than physical presence. You don't have to be a chaplain to do this. Practice "being fully present" in all your interactions. Start with a simple resolution today: Never to look at or play with your cell phone when you are interacting with another human!

9. Graceful

I met Anna for the first time on September 8, 2007. During that first visit, I felt a connection to her. She was warm, pleasant, friendly, gracious, welcoming, and was able to have a fairly coherent conversation. She told me that she had a wonderful life and spoke proudly about her six children and several grandchildren.

When I brought up the possible limitations of living in an assisted living facility, Anna surprised me with her response: "It is still a good life; I have never been unhappy in my life," she said.

I visit a lot of elderly patients who complain about the food, the monotony, the lack of attention from family etc. I visit 13 assisted living facilities, and it is a fact that most of the residents in many of those places are just miserable.

But Anna was an exception. During the nearly four years she has been on the hospice program, I have visited her numerous times. I have never seen her angry, unhappy, or unpleasant. I used to tell her that I could see the Holy Spirit in her, because she manifested the "Fruit of the Spirit" that apostle Paul talks about in Galatians chapter five: love, peace, joy, patience, kindness, goodness, faithfulness, gentleness, and self-control.

There is a bumper sticker that says: "If you have Jesus in your heart, notify your face." Many people claim that they believe in Jesus, but you don't see it in their demeanor or behavior. Anna always manifested the Christ within her through her friendly smile and peaceful demeanor.

As a hospice chaplain, I have to broach the subject of death at some point. Many of our patients are afraid or unwilling to talk about it. There are family members who ask me not to talk to mom or dad about dying. Some have requested me to remove my badge that says *hospice* on it because "it would frighten" them.

Anna was not afraid of death. She talked openly about it, and said that she had no fear of dying because, "I will live in a different dimension."

I was pleasantly surprised she used the word *dimension*. Since Anna was a staunch Catholic, I expected her to say that she would live in heaven with God and heaven is usually described as a "place" with pearly gates, gold-paved streets, and singing angels. *Dimension* is a more of a "state" than a "place."

Anna was confirming my notion about after-life, more as being in a *dimension* rather than being in a *place.* According to *String Theory*, there are ten dimensions to this universe. During our physical lives, we live in a three-dimensional world, with very little awareness of other dimensions. The "different dimension" that Anna was talking about is another word for heaven that could be right here on earth, not in a faraway place beyond the clouds.

Is it possible that Jesus was talking about that *dimension* when he said: "The Kingdom of God is in the midst of you," or when he said, "there are many *mansions* in my Father's house," did he mean *dimensions*? Is it possible that when he asked us to pray "Thy Kingdom come on earth as it is in heaven" he was reminding us to create and experience heaven on earth?

Anna seemed to believe that, and behaved as if it is the truth.

* * *

Ponder and Practice

> Do you believe that every human being is endowed with the *Divine Spirit*? If so, how do you explain sin and evil in the world?

> Among the *Fruit of the Spirit* listed—love, peace, joy, patience, kindness, goodness, faithfulness, gentleness and self-control—how many do you think you have in your life?

> If you were to change your notion of heaven from being a *"mansion* upstairs," to a *"dimension* right here," how will that impact your life and your relationships with the living and the dead?

10. Heaven's Back Door

It takes a special person to do what you do. I have heard that remark so many times while I am at the bedside of a dying patient or in a house comforting family members after the death of a loved one. The honest truth is that such remarks do not evoke any sense of grandiosity within me because, I believe that every person is special in what he or she does.

For example, I believe that the home health aides on my hospice team who change the pee-and-poop-soaked-diapers of the elderly patients are very special people. I admire their tenacity and dedication in doing such an extremely difficult job. I tell them that I would not be able to do what they do even if I am offered a thousand dollars to change one such diaper. But every one of the aides on my team, engages in personal care of at least six patients a day, with ease and grace. One aide told me that she looks forward to taking care of her patients, and she wouldn't do any other job. She has been a hospice aide for sixteen years!

The plumber who can figure out the problem with my toilet and make it work, is special. The mail man who has to stop his truck in front of 145 mail boxes in my housing complex, and extend his hand twice to each mail box—once to open the box and once to toss in the mail—is doing a very special and hard job. The toll it takes on his eyes while sorting thousands of pieces of mail each day, is unimaginable for me. The pilot who takes me from one country to another in that gigantic airplane is special. The clerk at the grocery store who checks out my grocery, is special. The guy at the gym who walks around with a towel, and wipes down sweat-soaked exercise machines, is special. Maid Martha, who diligently cleans the bathrooms in my office building every day, is special.

In my world, there are no un-special people or unimportant jobs.

I am blessed however, with one special perk in my job which no other job on earth has—accompanying another human being to the Gates of Heaven.

I am thinking of Liz, who had requested that I remain at her bedside during her final hours. Her daughter had special instructions to call me to the house when those hours approached.

It was a bright Thursday morning. Liz was non-responsive. I sat next to her bed, and her daughter sat on the other side. As her breaths became less frequent, and shallow, I had a feeling that the moment was approaching. I took Liz's hand in mine and whispered words of comfort and reassurance to her—happy thoughts for a journey back home into the heart of God. Within minutes, Liz took her last breath. When the life energy exited her physical body, it was instantly transformed, and turned into a celestial entity which I call an "angel."

That Thursday morning, I added one more angel to the long list of celestial companions who are watching over me, guiding me, and blessing me.

The Vitas hospice program in Broward County serves about 1700 patients a day. We have about five hundred deaths a month. I am not at the bedside of most of them. But every month, I get to be at the bedside of at least a dozen patients who are served by my team. These are men and women whom I unconditionally loved and cared for while they were alive. I had the chance of being with them, talking with them, holding their hands, and praying with them. I have witnessed many tearful and grateful eyes gazing at me at the end of a prayer, non-verbally thanking me for being with them at that special, final moment.

These are human beings whom I loved and they loved me back. My love for them does not cease when they are deceased and theirs don't either. In fact, now that they are angels, they are able to love me and bless me in abundant ways.

I clearly remember a special gift that patient Pauline promised me last year. Pauline was 85 years old and she was legally blind. But she had this uncanny ability to recognize my voice as soon as I entered her apartment. "Is that pastor Paul?" she would ask in her sweet gentle voice. She was a staunch Baptist and literally believed in the Bible. Even though we didn't see eye-to-eye on our biblical views, I loved Pauline for her simple faith and gentle spirit. Few months before her death, she told me:

"You know Pastor Paul, you have been so good to me all these months. I am going to do something good for you when I die and go to heaven."

I was curious and delighted to hear what she was going to do for me.

"I will leave heaven's back door open for you."

I am still planning to enter through the "front door."

However, in case there is a glitch at the last moment, and my plan doesn't pan out, or if St. Peter happens to be in a bad mood that day, it is always good to have a back-up plan.

No other job has that kind of perk!

* * *

Ponder and Practice

> "There are millions of people *working for you* to make your life possible each day." Unpack the meaning of that statement.

> Look at the following job pairings: pilot/plumber, cardiologist/cashier,manager/maid,surgeon/sweeper, CEO/chauffeur. If you categorize them as "higher" and "lower" jobs, you are thinking superficially. They are different roles, not diminished status.

> Make a conscious effort not to compare your job with anybody else's job. Think of five ways to make your job special.

11. Heart Breaking

One day, I was asked by my manager to go a house where a patient had just died. All I had was the name of the patient and the home address. I walked into a home that looked like a rehab facility, with a Hoyer Lift in the living room, a wheelchair in the corner and a physical therapy machine in the family room. I thought they all belonged to the patient who had just passed. Her name was Judy and she was 78.

The body lay on a medical bed in the corner of the living room, and her face was covered with a white linen. I offered condolences to Judy's daughter Lucy, who seemed like a take-charge kind of person. She was busy cleaning the rooms, getting rid of medications, and doing chores. After saying a prayer for Judy and calling the funeral home, I sat down with Lucy to talk about her mother.

Judy was diagnosed with pancreatic cancer a year ago. Lucy brought her mother home and took care of her until the end, providing the best care she could. The story about her mother Judy quickly turned into a story about her daughter Emily—a harrowing story of sadness, pain and loss, but also of inspiration, faith, resilience, brokenness, and wholeness, all combined in a saga of tragedy, trauma, and transformation.

On a Monday morning in 2008, Emily was excited to drive to school with her friend. Her father had allowed her to drive his car. Emily had just gotten her driver's license the Thursday before. Three miles away from home, she got into a serious accident and ended up in hospital with severe brain injury. Her friend escaped with minor injuries.

Emily was in a coma for three months. After being in three hospitals and two rehabs, Emily was finally brought home ten months after the accident. During her hospital days, Lucy quit her job and became a full time caregiver.

Emily was a thriving teenager, a good student, and a fashion model with high hopes and dreams. Today she sits at home in a wheelchair wearing diapers, can hardly talk, and has round-the-clock aides.

During the months and years following her accident, her parents grew apart. Her father Ken "could not handle" the situation. His sorrow led him to self-medicate which led to prescription pill related issues. He is separated from his wife, and was of no support to her either emotionally or financially. The house went into foreclosure. They filed for bankruptcy.

I was touched by Lucy's devotion to her daughter, and her untiring dedication to find ways to make Emily feel better. I was inspired by her faith, humbled by her positive attitude, and amazed by her stamina. My aches and pains vanished. My issues and complaints about life melted away. I felt ashamed about sweating silly stuff. I was blessed with another opportunity to ground myself.

I was curious to find out what helped Lucy to cope with hopelessness, and what sustained her through such a horrific tragedy.

She credits her strength to Jesus. She began attending church a year before Emily had the accident. Lucy believes that God was preparing her to face the tragedy that was just around the corner. Her life is based on the promises of Jesus in the Bible. She believes that God is with her every moment and He will help her get through this. "The Lord never gives me more than I can handle," she said. She is praying for a miracle for her daughter, and doing everything in her power to make life better for Emily.

Before leaving, I had a little chat with Emily, whose face shined with sheer joy. She asked me for a hug. I gave her a warm hug, kissed her on the forehead, and offered a silent prayer for her recovery.

Myself being the parent of a disabled son, individuals like Emily break my heart with sadness, and at the same time, mends it with gladness—a rare combination of raw life as it is experienced and lived on planet earth.

That day, I was touched, humbled, inspired, amazed, and of course, blessed by the deep faith of a devoted mother, and the graceful smile of a young woman. Their life journeys took a tragic detour seven years ago, and they are still in the *cul-de-sac* of uncertainty.

And yet, hope springs eternal in the hearts of this mother and daughter.

* * *

Ponder and Practice

> Faith seems to be the abiding anchor to Lucy's resilience in the midst of this terrific tragedy. Why do some people lose faith when they experience tragedies?

> Have you experienced a life-altering tragedy? If so, how did you deal with it? If you know someone who has/had such an experience, invite that person to share how s/he deals with it.

> Next time you have a challenging life-experience, re-frame it as a *blessing* instead of a *tragedy,* and see what happens. It may be hard to do that, but *words matter.* Words evoke feelings, feelings generate attitudes, and attitudes create behaviors.

12. History and Mystery

Marie is a 92 year old widow who was placed in an assisted living facility by her daughter because of her "forgetfulness" and declining eyesight. She was still mentally alert. Marie is unhappy at the facility which she describes as a "nuthouse." She was raised in the Baptist church by her strict father who did not allow her to read or dance which were her passions. Instead, she had to attend church twice a week and she felt that religion was "crammed down on her throat." She referred to her being raised in the "dunkers' church" and there was no love lost between Marie and her church.

I was a little anxious visiting Marie because the nurse had described her as a "bitch on wheels." The nurse also told me that this is one of those patients who "loves God and hates people." Although that was reason for a little anxiety, I have had several encounters with "difficult patients" that turned out to be surprisingly positive experiences.

During my visit, Marie was rigid in her demeanor and constricted in her responses. It was apparent that she wanted to be in control. She was angry and bitter. Although she said that her "children have their own lives," she was angry that they don't visit her enough. Marie was a self proclaimed "loner," who had a "chip on her shoulder" and an "attitude." As a result, she looked down upon people and thought of herself better than others. It is a very counter-productive attitude in the environment of an assisted living facility where socialization is the norm. She complains about "not having any friends," yet she seemed to be unaware of the dictum: "If you want a friend, be one."

I felt bad about Marie who had to spend her last days, isolated, alone, and mostly confined to her room. I grew up in a culture where joint-family system is still the norm. Assisted Living Facilities and Nursing Homes are a rarity in India. Parents live with their children until their death. Elders without children are usually taken care of by extended family. The elderly are revered and respected. Children consider it their duty to take care of their parents.

I recognize that warehousing the elderly in old age homes is an inevitable side effect of industrialization. However, working with these individuals who are largely ignored by society and sometimes abandoned by families, is always heart breaking.

My overwhelming compassion for the elderly always trumps any perceived rudeness on their part because, when I am with them, I am beholding history and mystery. I consider my elderly patients who have gone through the depression, the world wars and many other unfathomable life altering experiences, as mysteries to be contemplated and miracles to be experienced. I see 92 year old Marie as a conglomerate of persons, events, and experiences so vast to comprehend and too many to count. Therefore, despite her perceived rough exterior, I felt compassion for Marie because I believe that beneath that tough shell, there is a little girl waiting to emerge and connect.

I was not thrilled that Marie did not allow me to pray with her. "No, you say your prayer and I say my prayers. I know you are a nice person, but prayer is private," she said. Years ago, I would have been offended by such a reaction as a challenge to my pastoral authority. As a Catholic priest in India, I would have never gotten such a reaction from a patient, especially from a woman.

In the beginning of my ministry as a hospice chaplain, such reactions from patients have bothered me to the extent of re-mourning the loss of my priesthood. Those were the days when I used to live my life largely *outside-in*—reacting to outside stimuli mindlessly.

The more I have learned to live my life *inside-out*—responding to outside stimuli mindfully, these experiences of rejection of my apparent "pastoral authority" don't bother me anymore. I am aware of the fact that patient-preference comes first, and doing rituals and offering prayers contrary to their liking can only be counter-productive. It is also a great lesson in humility.

* * *

Ponder and Practice

> There is a saying that "majority of our problems are self-created." Make a list of of your perceived problems and see who is responsible for them, you? Or others?

> I have heard that human beings are like ice-bergs—with only ten percent visible above the surface. Yet we seem to judge people based on what is visible on the outside. Let us be aware of that unjust and unfair practice.

> Are you a curious person? Curious about people, places, and life in general? Your happiness will rise if you raise your level of curiosity. In the classroom of life, we should all be like kindergarten kids, with our hands up, all the time!

13. Atheist

George is an 88 year old white male who was admitted into hospice care for cardiovascular disease. When I called his daughter to let her know that I would be visiting her dad, Pam told me that her dad was an atheist and that he may not welcome my visit. I decided to visit him anyway, partly out of curiosity and partly out of my desire to visit all patients on my team. I am curious about the God that the atheists don't believe in, because most likely I don't believe in that God either.

George was the resident of an assisted living facility. He was unhappy with the environment, and unimpressed by the mediocre service he received from the staff. He wanted to get out of there if he could, but felt helpless because his daughter was in charge. He was bothered by a wound that was causing him some pain which made it impossible to get comfortable.

George was a smart man, pleasant and friendly, with a good sense of humor. He was also depressed and lonely because he was confined to his room and dealing with pain—both physical and emotional. He was curt and brazen in his attitude, and he did not mince words. He spoke his mind and I liked it.

"Did you say you are a chaplain...but I am an atheist; does that make me a bad person?" he asked. When I replied, "I don't think so," George continued: "For 63 years I went to church with my wife. I have read some parts of the Bible...I think it is a lot of baloney."

There are a lot of contradictions in the bible, I chimed in. "How come you went to church and listened to those stories, all those years?"

"I went with her to make her happy. I don't believe in that crap. I think people believe those things because they are afraid."

George spoke without filters, and the fact that I did not act shocked about some of his statements seemed to make him comfortable to speak his mind.

Sometimes I listen to 89.3 FM, a local religious radio station. I listen mostly for "entertainment" because I laugh out loud when I hear fundamentalist preachers make statements like these: "God could have saved Jesus from dying on the cross. There were seventy two thousand angels standing ready to get him off the cross; but they were under strict orders from God the Father not to interfere, because if Jesus did not die, we would not be saved."

I am sure George was referring to such nonsensical talk in churches which he described as "baloney." I identified with him and he seemed to find an ally in me. I believe that the Bible is the "word of God in the words of men" with all their limitations—cultural, religious, and historical—which helps me to minister to patients with faith or no faith.

Even though he did not believe in what the preachers said, the fact that George went to church with his wife to make her happy touched a special chord in me. I attend church not because I believe everything my fellow-Christians believe or agree with everything I hear from the pulpit. I attend church because I want to be with my wife and children who love to be in church every Sunday. They are happy that I am with them and that is important to me regardless of the fact that we believe differently.

George helped me confirm my conviction that "my life is not all about me." He also reminded me about the importance of providing non-judgmental ministry in non-denominational settings. Years ago, when I worked in the confines of the Catholic Church, an atheist would have bothered me both theologically and spiritually. I would have branded him "wrong" and "unworthy of heaven."

I have traveled so far from those ideological positions, and have come to realize that God has no preference as to what we "believe" or whether or not we believe at all, as long as we "behave."

* * *

Ponder and Practice

> An atheist may not be against God but against the traditional "understanding" of God. Next time you meet an atheist, ask him/her to tell you about the God s/he doesn't believe in.

> Let these words of Carl Jung help you move away from childish beliefs about God, religion and life itself: *Thoroughly unprepared, we take the step into the afternoon of life. Worse still, we take this step with the false presupposition that our truths and our ideals will serve us as hitherto. But we cannot live the afternoon of life according to the program of life's morning, for what was great in the morning will be little at evening and what in the morning was true, at evening will have become a lie.*

> Some so-called atheists are better human beings than some so-called religious people. How does that fact prompt you to re-think your ideas about religion?

14. Wiped out

Joe is lying in his bed staring at the ceiling and repeating the phrase: "I was totally wiped out." He does not like where he is and what has become of his once-vibrant life.

Joe is 85 years old, twice divorced father of two adult children. Joe is not happy with what his children did to him by placing him in an assisted living facility and signing him up for hospice.

"I hate living with these old people," he says. Even though he is kind of "old," what sets him apart from other residents is his mobility and coherence. Unlike a majority of his fellow-residents, Joe is able to walk on his own, and is aware of what is going on.

The facility, located in a low-income neighborhood, is an old building, single floor, housing more than 250 residents. The carpet seems to be older than the building itself. The aroma and ambiance of this crowded, enclosed space is suffocating to Joe.

Until eight months ago, he was living on his own, in his townhouse. According to his daughter, he was not taking care of himself or taking care of the house. He began losing weight and his home became cluttered with stuff and contaminated with cockroaches. "It became a health hazard and I had to take him out of there," said his daughter. He couldn't take care of himself. His daughter was worried that his father was a "fall risk," and she didn't want to find him dead on the floor one day.

But Joe wants to hear none of it. He is angry that his independence is gone. He had to move into the assisted living facility with "the clothes on my back." He mourns the loss of his house, his car, his music videos, his records, his clothes, and his furniture. "I feel wiped out."

During every visit, Joe gives me a litany of complaints about everything he lost and the "cruelty" of his children. *They brought me here and took off, they don't come to visit me. Why did they do this to me? What did I do wrong? I could have lived in my house. I could have driven my own car. Now, I have to depend on others to go anywhere. I am not even free to go outside of this building for some fresh air, without somebody watching me; this is like a jail and it smells, too.*

Joe is miserable, unrealistic, and irrational. He is fiercely resisting reality, and it is very hard to convince him of the wisdom of living in a place where help is available.

I believe that an antidote to misery is rational thinking. A rational analysis of his mental deficits and health needs should convince him of his need for living in an assisted living facility. I tried but Joe is not convinced. He has a counter argument for every one of my suggestions. He blames his children for "wiping him out." He is angry at the world. He is unaccepting of the pain in his arthritic knees and unwelcoming of his advanced age. "I want things to go back to normal just as it was before," he says.

This is an argument neither his children nor this chaplain can win. His children are frustrated. They feel helpless. Dad's unabated complaints have made visits unpleasant for them. "Nothing is getting through to the thick skull of the old man," an angry daughter once told me. She was giving voice to the anger and frustrations of caregivers of the elderly everywhere.

As chaplain, I tried to appeal to his religious faith. Joe is a staunch Catholic and he was very active in church. He was the head usher for his parish for many years. He would arrive at the church fifteen minutes before Mass, dressed in suit with his name tag proudly displayed on his lapel. He greeted people as they entered the church and showed them to their pews. "He was a showman and he loved it," said his daughter.

One day when his depressive rumination reached its crescendo, I gently tapped on his shoulder and said: "Joe, you have been a Catholic all along; you attended Mass every Sunday; what about your faith? Is it helping you at this stage of your life?"

"I did that thing for prestige," he said. Being the head usher at the parish church was prestigious for Joe. Faith apparently had nothing much to do with it then, nor is it impacting him now.

Joe did not age gracefully. He died unhappy. His children felt helpless. Unfortunately, more people age and die like Joe. I don't think caregivers can do much except, accept this difficult stage in their lives and love their loved ones, unconditionally.

* * *

Ponder and Practice

> As a young man, Joe appears to have lived his life using his muscle strength rather than his mind. There is no indication that he engaged in critical thinking or conscious living during his younger days. How are you navigating your life?

> Joe is not aging gracefully. What are some of the things you can do today so that when you get to Joe's age, you will process reality differently and experience life joyfully?

> Remember to focus on your *thinking* because all your experiences are processed in your mind. *Our minds create our reality.* In fact there is no external reality that is not created first, in the mind.

15. Bad Start in Religion

Seventy two year old Tommy was living a care-free life on a boat in the Bahamas. He had no living relatives anywhere that he was aware of. When his eyesight became an issue, Tommy went to the doctor for a check-up and found out to his horror that he had lung cancer. As Tommy was not interested in pursuing treatment, the doctor suggested hospice care.

I took an instant liking for this gentle spirit who was left alone in the middle of the sea of life with no rudders or helpers. A court-appointed guardian took care of his affairs, but she had no time to spent with Tommy as she was bombarded with many other similar cases.

Tommy had a rough childhood. His parents separated when he was five years old. An alcoholic father drank himself to death when Tommy was in high school. Mom, who was devastated by an early divorce, did not have the skills or the wherewithal to take care of Tommy. She dropped Tommy off at his grandma's house and left for good. He was just five years old. Grandma didn't have much to offer Tommy except a roof over his head and three meals a day.

When Tommy realized I was a chaplain, he said: "I am not a religious guy." He knew chaplains' role because during his four years in the Air Force, he had heard that word. "I never had to go a chaplain for anything," he said. "I had a bad start in religion," he added.

I was determined to make his last encounter with religion a positive experience. It is a fact that many people have been hurt, judged, alienated, excluded, and punished by religion. I want to be a proxy for good religion, especially for my patients in whose life I possibly can make a difference. So I listened intently to Tommy's story of his "bad start in religion."

There was a church walking distance from my grandmother's house. My grandma didn't go to church, but she thought I should.

This grandma obviously didn't know that religion is caught rather than taught.

She dressed me up in nice clothes and sent me to the church. I walked there, and when I entered the church, I saw a guy who looked like Ichabod Crane (a Disney character*) at the pulpit which scared the hell out of me. He was yelling and screaming about the punishment waiting those who are bad. When I sat down on the floor in front of the pulpit, the preacher suddenly stopped. Pointing his fingers at me, he said: "You don't belong here, you should be in bible study class down stairs" and pointed to the door leading to the the basement of the church. I bolted from the church and went downstairs to the class already in session. The teacher was not happy that I walked in late. I remember her talking about Moses but I didn't understand any of it. So, I walked back home. Grandma was upset that I had returned home before "church ended" and took me back. It was a traumatic experience.*

In high school, grandma signed me up for catechism but I didn't buy into much of it...I took the communion "cracker" but it didn't mean much...I have never been impressed by organized religion.

My heart was filled with compassion for Tommy. He was visibly sad about the life he had lived because he told me that he was not proud about some of the things he had done, and was embarrassed to talk about it.

I told him that regardless of what he had done, God still loved him unconditionally. For Tommy, my words were "unbelievable," yet he seemed to be relieved, albeit, momentarily.

At the end of our visit, I offered to say a prayer with him. "It feels awkward, because I have never prayed in public or much in private for that matter," he said. I told him that he didn't have to say anything except close his eyes and relax. We held hands and these words followed:

Gracious Lord, I join my fellow human being and brother, Tommy this morning and raise our awareness to your loving presence in us and around us. I thank you for the gift of life for each of us and lift up to you Tommy whom you created in your image and likeness 72 years ago. He is having a rough time these days. I pray that you hold him in the palm of Your hands as You have always done, all these years. I pray that You calm his fears, wipe his tears, and hold his hands as he walks through the Valley of the Shadow of Death. Be with him in his moments of sadness and loneliness and comfort him with your mercy, forgiveness, and compassion, today, tomorrow, and forever, amen.

Tommy's eyes bubbled with tears and I had tears of joy for the opportunity to be with another human being during one of the lowest points of his life and lift his spirit, even for a moment.

* * *

Ponder and Practice

> Did you ever have a similar experience like Tommy's? How did you deal with that?

> According to a recent survey, 34 percent of millennials identify themselves as "nones" (having no religious affiliation). What does that say about religion in America?

> If you think that posting the *Ten Commandments* in public buildings, and saying *Merry Christmas* instead of *Happy Holidays* are important, you are likely to be superficially religious. Please focus on the *Beatitudes* and the *Sermon on the Mount* rather than the *Ten Commandments!*

16. Rejection

Chaplain Paul, is there any way you could visit patient Molly tomorrow because she has been very anxious and afraid the last couple of days. When I got that text from my team nurse on a Sunday night, I was only glad to oblige because that is my *raison d'etre* for being a hospice chaplain.

Monday morning, I eagerly drove to the assisted living facility where Molly lived. As I entered her room, I was greeted by her daughter Sally, who was sitting quietly, watching her mother sleep peacefully. Sally seemed relieved to see me. I gave her a hug and acknowledged the feelings and emotions associated with watching one's mother waste away.

Molly is 85 years old. She has been a widow for 15 years. In the last six months, her health has been declining, and she was no more able to engage in activities of daily living—ADLs in hospice parlance. Her appetite diminished and her ability to walk declined rapidly. Molly was confined to her bed and her wheelchair. Of late, she has been sleeping most of the day.

Molly had told her five children that she did not want to prolong her life in less than favorable conditions. She made preparations for her exit by arranging for her own funeral years ago. She told Sally that she had lived long enough, and was ready to meet the Lord and greet her husband, who is waiting for her in heaven.

A Few days earlier, Sally noticed a change in her mother's otherwise peaceful attitude and demeanor. She seemed very anxious, and told Sally that she was afraid to close her eyes for fear of dying in her sleep.

Sally thought it would be a good idea for the chaplain to visit and talk to her mother, pray with her, and hopefully help ease her anxiety.

After offering support and reassurance to Sally for a few minutes, I suggested that I would give her mother the sacrament of the sick, formerly known as the *Last Rites*. Although she was a non-practicing Catholic in the last decade, I thought Molly would appreciate the sacrament and the grace it brought. I also offered to give her mother a rosary which she could use for additional spiritual solace.

As I left the room to get the holy oil, the holy water and the rosary from my car, Sally called her sister Mindy who lived in Chicago, and put her on the speaker phone, so that she could also participate in the sacrament and pray with and for her ailing mother.

When I returned to the room, Molly was wide awake. Sally was sitting at the edge of her mother's bed, holding her hand. I approached Molly from the other side of the bed, identified myself, and asked if she would like to receive the sacrament.

Molly turned her head towards me with a harsh stare and said: "I am not interested in Church; so don't talk to me about it. You can now leave the room."

Instantly, I picked up the holy oil and the holy water bottle I had placed at the edge of the bed, and quietly left the room. Sally was embarrassed beyond words and didn't look at me. I heard Mindy at the other end of the phone: "Oh, my God."

I told Sally that I would wait outside the room in the lobby area, and that she was welcome to come out if she needed to talk.

I sat there and began writing my notes. A few minutes later, Sally came out of the room and said she had to feed her mother and suggested that I leave my card so that she could call me later.

In fifteen years of hospice ministry, I have never seen such a stern, negative, almost diabolic reaction from a patient approaching death. There was something about the eyes of this patient that I couldn't figure out—a ferocious fury swirling around her eyeballs. Why would she react with such disdain for a sacrament that could have brought her some peace? What must have triggered such an emotional reaction to a representative of the Church? Is it possible that she had a bad experience with Church? I would never know.

In the early years of my ministry, an experience like this would have thrown me off my game. I would have doubted my personal abilities and second-guessed my pastoral efficacy. I would have hidden under the depressive blanket of recrimination and self doubt for days, but not anymore.

I refuse to let other's ignorance become my insomnia and other's baggage my burden. I have learned not to let other's insensitivity trigger my insecurity or other's troubles tarnish my tranquility. The tool that helps me cope easily with such experiences—which are extremely rare—is the awareness that situations like these are above my pay grade. This is the domain of the Divine and all I need to do is get out of the way.

I do not pretend therefore to understand the emotions lurking in the inner recesses of Molly's mind. Nor do I attempt to interpret the unknown. However, I could not help scan the Scriptures for similar scenarios. What came to mind were the words of Jesus to his disciples as he sent them off to preach: "And if any place will not welcome you or listen to you, shake the dust off your feet when you leave..." (Mark 6:11)

I said a quiet prayer for Molly that she find grace, peace, and healing for whatever might be ailing her, and went to visit my next patient.

* * *

Ponder and Practice

> Think of an episode where you had an experience of rejection. Re-live that experience using the "Who, what, when, where, how" formula.

> Live your life "inside-out" rather than "outside-in." *You feel good not because the world is right, but your world is right, because you feel good.* ~Wayne Dyer

> Live consciously and become UNFUCKWITHABLE—a state of being truly at peace, and in touch with yourself, and nothing anyone says or does bothers you, and no negativity or drama can touch you!

17. D.O.B. 2-13-15

Wendy always slept with her cell phone next to her pillow because she knew that when your dad is 101 years old and living in an assisted living facility, there could be an emergency at any time.

Eddy was born in Brooklyn on February 13, 1915. He owned a butcher shop, and raised a family of five children, two boys and three girls, through hard work. His wife Barbara stood by him through their 67 years of marriage until her death in 1995.

For the past twenty years Eddy has been a widower, but an active widower who participated in all the activities at his assisted living facility. He played Bingo on Thursdays, danced to the Karaoke songs on Fridays, played cards with his buddies, and went out once a week for lunch with fellow residents.

It was all going well until six months ago, when he had a fall, and since then he had been confined to a wheelchair. He also had to wear adult diapers as he could not get to the bathroom on time and by himself. His eyesight began to fade and his hearing increasingly deteriorated.

As his ability to cope with ADLs diminished, Wendy hired an aide to be with her father for 12 hours a day. Now, ADL—an acronym that is commonly used in assisted living facilities, means Activities of Daily Living—such as getting up from bed, brushing one's teeth, shaving, showering, getting dressed, eating, and everything else one must do without assistance from others.

Eddy was extremely resistant to the idea of an aide—a middle aged woman from Jamaica—staying with him in his room all day, every day. He was very uncomfortable about the aide putting diapers on him and changing him when wet. He didn't like the idea of sponge baths. He felt his dignity being violated when she fed him in the dining room, and other residents were watching.

Eddy complained to his daughter about his abiding aide. He was not happy to lose his freedom and independence.

But Wendy, who was worried about her father's safety, insisted on having the aide so that she could go home in peace knowing that her dad was safe. She didn't feel comfortable leaving her dad alone in a room on the third floor of the ALF. What if her dad—after entering the room and closing the door, fainted or fell—not an unlikely event in the case of a 101 year old man. Or what if he slipped and fell when he went to the bath room? Wendy was keenly aware of the fact that "fall" is the greatest risk for the elderly in this country. At age 101, Eddy was a perfect candidate for fall risk. Wendy could not imagine the thought of finding her dad incapacitated or dead in his room.

On August 14, 2015, Eddy fell off his bed and lost consciousness. The aide panicked and called 911. Within minutes, the ambulance arrived, and Eddy was transported to the nearest hospital. The aide informed Wendy about it, and she drove to the hospital to meet her dad there.

The day that Wendy dreaded seemed to have arrived. She drove through busy streets, wondering and worrying if this would be the day for him to join his wife. When she reached the emergency room, Eddy was already in triage. She had to fill out some papers before she could go in. She took the clip board from the clerk, filled out the information, and gave it back to the clerk.

The clerk looked at the clipboard, and then looked at Wendy and said: "I'm so sorry; he is a baby, just few months old; is it your grand-son?"

"Grandson? What do you mean?" retorted an irritated Wendy.

"It says here that his date of birth is 2-13-15."

That is when Wendy's anger turned into amusement. Her father was born on 2-13-1915. She realized that she could not blame the clerk entirely, because she should have been more specific about the year of birth. They both laughed out loud.

The irony is that Wendy's "mistake" is not actually a mistake. Clarifying her dad's year of birth with a four-digit number—1915—may be necessary for practical purposes, but in reality, the two-digit year that Wendy wrote and the clerk read, is actually closer to the truth in Eddy's situation today.

Eddy who is 101 years old fits the profile of a baby except for his looks and body weight. He is like a baby in many aspects. He needs help getting up from bed. He needs to be washed. He wears a diaper. He needs help brushing his teeth, taking a shower, and getting dressed. He needs to be fed. He needs supervision. He needs to be protected from falling down, and needs to be picked up when he falls. He is dependent on his aide, like a baby is dependent on his mother.

Eddy is going through his second childhood, a prospect many of my patients detest and their caregivers dread.

Shakespeare was right: "Once a man, twice a child."

* * *

Ponder and Practice

> Let's do a "word association game." Write down seven words associated with your idea of "nursing homes." Explain the feelings behind those words.

> Do a fantasy meditation, imagining yourself to be a resident in a nursing home.

> It is 9 a.m. You are still in bed. Your eyes are open. But your body cannot move. You are wearing a diaper filled with urine and excrement. You are waiting for help. This is the reality for millions of elderly among us. Say a "gratitude prayer" today if you are able to get up in the morning and do your ADLs. (Activities of Daily Living)

47

18. Misery Loves Company

Marjorie is miserable. She spreads her misery around by being critical of the staff at the assisted living facility. According to her, the nurses are incompetent, the kitchen is dirty, and the housekeeping staff do not know anything about keeping the house clean. She has alienated her family too, having accused them of "sticking her in a hell hole" and leaving.

Marjorie spends her days and nights inside her room. She gets out only to go to the dining room for three meals a day. She does not participate in any recreational activities. Her antipathy towards fellow residents is understandable in that most of them are incapable of engaging in meaningful conversations. They sit around all day staring at the walls or sleeping. Marjorie still has her faculties and she cannot bear the thought of associating with "those old people."

Two days after she was admitted to our hospice team, I visited Marjorie. I had no prior warnings about the unique personality of this patient. The report from an admission nurse focused mainly on the medical history, with no information about her psycho-social background.

I entered her room and greeted her. She was reading the newspaper. She raised her head and looked at me with a hostile gaze, and inquired who was "barging" into her room. When I introduced myself as the hospice chaplain, her face turned red and she became agitated.

"I am not expecting any visitors and I have nothing to talk about," she said. I lingered a bit hoping to soften her up with small talk—but to no avail. "You can leave now or I am leaving," she said.

Since I didn't move fast enough for her, she got up from her chair and walked towards the door.

I left her room feeling sad, wondering about the possible negative experiences that paved the foundation for Marjorie's life. Human beings don't automatically become sarcastic in their tone, sardonic in their attitude or hostile towards others for no apparent reason. Nobody suddenly succumbs to sullenness or become suspicious of their surroundings overnight. There is always a rugged road of abuse, pain, or abandonment that they have traversed before getting to a point of such anger and anhedonia. I was curious. So I called her daughter Lisa, hoping that she could shed light on her mother's personality.

Lisa started out by saying that her mother has "abandonment issues." She didn't go into detail but described her mother as an "aggressive person who is always looking for an argument." She has accused the ALF staff of putting poison in her food. "Mom has become excessively hostile in the last five years while her disease is getting progressively worse," she added. Lisa is "tired and exhausted," taking care of her mother, and told me that it would be a "relief" when she dies. At the end of our conversation, Lisa apologized to me on her mother's behalf for the "rough treatment" I had received from her mother.

As far as I am concerned, no apology was necessary because I was not offended by Marjorie's response or reaction. I would never pretend to know what might be going on in people's lives to respond or react in a particular way at any given time. I have come to realize that when others react negatively towards me, it is more about what they are going through than about me. This approach of not making others' baggage my burden has helped me cope better with a variety of unwelcome situations in life.

Regardless of Marjorie's first response, I was not ready to give up on her. It doesn't take any special effort on my part to try again to visit her because she lives in an ALF where I have other patients. So, I went to see her a second time. Marjorie surprised me with a pleasant demeanor and invited me in.

She wanted to make sure I didn't stay long, but shared a bit about her early life in Michigan, her career as a school teacher, and her two deceased husbands. We were making progress because I was not thrown out of the room. I had a feeling she was warming up to me, albeit very gingerly, and I gently validated her feelings of loneliness and abandonment in a home that is "designed for people waiting to die."

My third visit to Marjorie went much smoother than the first two, considering that I was thrown out of her room two months earlier. Her defenses were down, and her paranoia had subsided. Her comfort level had risen, and Marjorie openly shared about the struggles of raising her two adopted children—a fact that she was reluctant to disclose before. She even told me that her son had served jail time—an "embarrassing event for a mother to talk about."

Marjorie talked about some painful experiences of her life, often daubing tears, and I thought it was time to broach the subject of God who may or may not have helped her cope with the challenges of her life. She told me that she was born and raised *Methodist* but has not been influenced or impacted by any kind of religion. As an adult, she tried the *Unitarian Church* "to make friends." "I am not sure about this God thing," she said.

"You are valuable in God's eyes, even if He is not valuable in yours," I said.

Marjorie stared at me for a moment with a whimsical look.

"That's an interesting statement. I never thought about it that way," she said.

My statement seemed to cause cognitive dissonance for Marjorie who considered herself an atheist.

I told her to forget about her faithfulness to God, and focus on God's faithfulness to her. I also mentioned to her that those who are *looking* for God are actually looking for *Him* with *His* eyes!

My response to Marjorie came out of my deep conviction that God cares about us even when we don't care about God. I experience the God who knew me *before* I was even formed in my mother's womb. I believe that a human being denying God is like a fish denying the existence of water.

French theologian Blaise Pascal thinks that we are incapable of reaching out to God, unless God reaches out to us first. His powerful words, always gives me the spiritual chills:

"You would not seek *Me* if you hadn't already found *Me;* and you would not have found *Me*, if *I* had not found you first."

* * *

Ponder and Practice

> Make a list of the so called "difficult" people in your life. If the list has more than three names, you are likely to be a "difficult" person!

> Some people are easily offended. A wrong look from somebody can offend them. How sensitive is your "offense button?" List five things that offend you the most in this world.

> Imagine living in a world where nothing happens *to* you, but everything happens *through* you.

19. Vitas *versus* Vista

The name of the company I work for is called VITAS Health Care. *Vitas* is a Latin word which means, *life*. Although we are in the field of death and dying, we want the world to know that ultimately, we are about "quality of life" before death.

We go to business fairs and conventions to promote our company. A few years ago, I was at a church fair with other vendors. We had a nice table set up with literature about *Vitas*. We had pens and mugs and tea shirts with *Vitas* written all over them. We also had a huge banner that said: *Vitas Hospice.*

This nice lady walked up to my table and said: "I have a score to settle with your company." She was angry. She said that her husband was in hospice care for three months. He is now dead and buried, but she is getting bills from our company for thousands of dollars.

I told her that our company does not send out bills to any patient or families. If a patient is 65 years or older, *Medicare* covers hospice care. If a patient is under 65, private insurance picks up the tab. *Vitas* does not send bills to patients or families. That is a fact, and I told her that. She became more angry. She accused me of not knowing the policies and practices of my company. I was not amused. Being a professional, however, I did not show my emotion. She continued her barrage of complainst…and finally she opened her pocket book, took out an envelope and threw it on the table: "If you don't believe me, you look at them."

I picked up the envelope, took out the papers and looked. Yes, they were medical bills. Yes, they were for thousands of dollars and the amount, was past due....but there was a problem—a problem with just one misplaced letter of the alphabet.

Those bills were from an insurance company called VISTA. *VITAS* and *VISTA*—two different companies, one letter of the alphabet, a huge difference. Had she paid attention to it, a lot of headache could have been avoided that morning—the agitation, the anger, the ill-feeling, the racing heart beats, the high blood pressure, and of course, the embarrassment…and the profound apology.

There is a saying that *speed kills.* We see it on TV on a daily basis. People going 90 miles an hour lose control of the vehicle, hit the wall or tree or a truck, and die on the spot. Life in the fast lane can drain the life out of us physically, emotionally, and spiritually.

We live in a fast paced society surrounded by microwave ovens, ATM machines, smart phones, instant messaging, and of course multitasking, seeking instant gratification. We are so distracted, and frazzled, and always in a hurry, with no time or patience to stop and smell the flowers.

We become easily frustrated and severely impatient.

Slow down. Take a deep breath. Pay attention to your surroundings. Observe. Talk less. Listen more. And check twice before you press the "send" button on that electronic device!

* * *

Ponder and Practice

> Animals act on impulse and instinct. Humans are supposed to use imagination and intuition. Slow down and pay attention and pave the path for peaceful living.

> According to Neale Donald Walsch, "the world is in the condition it is in because the world is full of *sleep-walkers,* living in a dream and watching that dream turn into a nightmare." So, wake up and pay attention.

> Meditate for ten minutes in the morning and ten minutes before bed. Meditation helps with conscious living which can be an antidote to so many of our problems.

20. Awful *versus* Awesome

Eileen is a 91 year old patient served by our hospice team.

She was alert and oriented, and resting in bed. She was a proud woman who did not want to "air the dirty laundry" with me, but her son Jeff, who was "severely stressed out," wanted to talk.

During the two and a half hours of conversation, I had the privilege to peek into the pathological plight of a family, limping through life, for no good reason. Jeff described his family as "totally dysfunctional," filled with jealousy, hatred, and bitterness towards each other.

Three years ago, when his mother was no longer able to take care of her affairs, she appointed Jeff her Power of Attorney. This infuriated his siblings, Barry, Matt, Janice and Millie. They reportedly began ganging up on him. Nasty emails and phone calls were exchanged between the siblings. Jeff was accused of causing a heart attack for Janice, who apparently had to call 911 because she was so stressed out by the drama happening in their lives.

Jeff played two voice mail messages from Millie, calling him a liar and telling him that God would punish him in hell for what he was doing to the family.

One day, Barry visited his mother when Jeff was away. He wanted to take his mother to an attorney to make him the POA (Power of Attorney). His mother was furious because she did not want to be dragged from her death bed to an attorney's office.

The next day, she told Jeff that she did not want to die seeing her children fighting. So he sent an email to his siblings, inviting them to come for a reconciliation meeting. No one responded to that email. There is so much anger, jealousy, discontentment and pure animosity between the siblings. Their dying mother feels helpless, and wonders what she did wrong to deserve it.

This is just one example of thousands of individuals and families who are merely surviving and limping through life in this valley of tears, who are totally missing out on the fullness of life that is their birthright. Their default response to events and experiences is: life is *awful!*

Let me now introduce Veronica, who is six months away from her 100th birthday. She is also a patient served by my hospice team. Veronica is confined to her room in an assisted living facility where she has lived for the past eight years. She ambulates using a walker, is legally blind, but her mind is still sharp. She has been a widow for 45 years. Her two sons died of cancer in their fifties. She has two daughters-in-law and a grandson, living out of state. She has no money. All that she has is a bed, a commode, and a walker. She tells me that she is the "luckiest woman in the world." "God has blessed me from the top of my head to the tip of my toes," she often repeats. Veronica is always smiling, always happy, and always full of life. When I ask her about the *secret* of her happiness, Veronica tells me: "The secret is that it is not a secret. I just think happy thoughts." Veronica's default response is: life is *awesome!*

What separates the *awful* from the *awesome?* There is no **e** after the **w** in *awful* and that makes all the difference. The **e** is for *enlightenment* which also means *awakening*. When we sleep-walk through life, unconscious about, and unaware of the meaning and mystery of life, everything becomes awful. Enlightenment is not reserved for the Buddha or Jesus. It is ours to claim, if only we are willing to *wake up* and light the candle within. Add the **e** to your life and everything becomes full of awe—*awe-full* or, awesome.

I know there is no such word in the English language, but part of thriving in life is to "create" the kind of world we want to live in, using the imagination and creativity God has endowed us with. So, I choose to create a life and a world that is "awe-full," just as I am now creating a word *fantasticulous*, to describe an awesome life, by combining *fantastic* and *fabulous*.

Ponder and Practice

> Ninety percent of the problems in our lives are self-created. Engage in conscious living to bring down that percentage to ten, which represents problems "beyond your control."

> *Almost the whole world is asleep. Everybody you know, everything you see, everybody you talk to is sleeping...only a few people are awake, and they live in a state of total amazement.* (From the movie Joe *versus Volcano)*

> You came into this world pre-installed with the *Image of God,* or the *soul* which I call the *Amazement App.* Activate your *Amazement App,* by engaging in daily meditation. Imitate the *Chick-Fil-A* slogan: ***One App. Endless Awesome.***

21. Ceramic Cup

Ginny put on her pajamas and came out of the bathroom to realize—embarrassingly—that it was only 11 a.m. in the morning. She had just woken up from a nap in her easy chair after breakfast. When she woke up, she thought it was already close to midnight and went into the bathroom to change for bed. She was mortified that she got it so wrong and cursed her age.

I will be 99 in October...Oh what a terrible number...I hate it...I don't like it...that means life is over and I don't even want to think about what is coming next. Ginny whined and mourned as I began my visit with her.

"What do you think comes next?" I asked.

"I don't know, you tell me," she said.

Ginny was in total denial of her age, and fearful of the inevitable result of old age. I had several visits with Ginny in the past year, and had earned her trust to speak my mind. I told her that when one reaches into the nineties, death may be around the corner.

"Don't say that," she interjected immediately. "It is easy for you to say that, because you are so young."

I was happy to hear her say that I was young, because at 64, the only places I feel young, are assisted living facilities and nursing homes. I also feel young at the five o'clock hour in Florida restaurants where the elderly rush in for their early bird dinners. Not very comforting!

My little speech about the tentativeness of life, the inevitability of death, and the 29 bonus years added to her biblically perfect age of three scores and ten, had no impact on Ginny.

She continued: *Since I am 99, it makes me depend on other people. The girls here have to help me get dressed and I hate that. I want to do it myself. I don't look for anything else except that I feel good every day...is that too much to ask?*

I wanted to say, "Yes, at your age, it is too much to ask," but I didn't.

She continued: *I don't need any pain when I walk, I don't want to be in a wheel chair...that is so humiliating...I urinate too much...why is it happening to me...I don't like it.*

Ginny is a good example of a person who engages in the unrewarding exercise of caressing her ceramic cup of issues and problems. She is focused on her lack rather than her abundance. She has no awareness of the problems of the wider world.

The default position of my pastoral heart is always empathy, but I struggle to feel empathy for Ginny because she is totally unrealistic and ungrateful. Unlike many of my other patients, Ginny had a pretty good ride. She was happily married for 64 years until her husband died at age 93. She has two wonderful children, who are in their sixties, and doing well in life. She has two well-accomplished grand children and six great grandchildren. The walls in her room are adorned with photos of happy family members. Her daughter visits every Saturday to take her out for lunch. Ginny has told me many times: "Thank God I had no tragedies in my life."

I don't expect Ginny to be an optimist, although that would be the ideal. I would, however, very much like her to transcend her predominantly pessimistic attitude and become more realistic. I wish she acknowledged with gratitude that she had a great life—that 99 years of life on earth with most of it going right, is an unusual blessing; that at 99, aches and pains are endemic to existence, and that at 99 she should be glad that she is still on this side of the grave, *walking!*

I prayed with Ginny, and left hoping the Lord will open her heart wide towards gratefulness.

* * *

Ponder and Practice

> List some of the feelings that Ginny's story evokes in you. What does it say about who you are and how you deal with life's inevitable challenges?

> 1.2 billion people in the world do not have electricity. Eight hundred million people do not have access to clean water. Imagine living without power and clean water for the rest of your life. Close your eyes, and think about all the implications of that dark, dry reality.

> Meditate on the meaning of the saying: "I cried because I had no shoes until I met a man who had no feet."

22. Cosmic Container

Tom is a 96 year old patient on my team diagnosed with COPD (Chronic Obstructive Pulmonary Disorder). He becomes out of breath walking from the bedroom to the living room. The oxygen tubes attached to his nostrils follow him wherever he goes in the apartment. When he goes out, the oxygen tank is behind his wheelchair.

During my visits, Tom, a WW II veteran of the US Navy, sits up, and is happy to tell me stories of his Navy life. Life is not easy for him these days. His four daughters live in other states. He has a private aide to help him with cooking and cleaning, for a few hours a day.

"Life is an effort for me, and I am at the death-phase of my life," he said with a deep sigh. "But who am I kidding? I had a good life; I have no regrets. I had a wonderful wife and four great daughters. I hope I am going to heaven."

"Anyone complaining about aches and pains, and un-cooperating body parts don't have my sympathies; it is called life, deal with it," he added.

I commented Tom for his positive outlook on life while being deprived of the most basic need in life—the ability to breathe freely.

I sat at the feet of this venerable veteran, wanting to hear more about his positive philosophy of life.

Let me tell you something," he began: *I accept my situation because fighting it is not going to make it any better. Acceptance comes from the awareness that nothing lasts forever. This body is temporary. Nothing in this world lasts forever.*

"What should I tell my patients who find it so hard to accept their frailty and finality? I asked.

"Let them sail to the South Pacific," he said.

"What do you mean?"

He recalled an experience as a young navy man at the South Pacific.

Standing on the deck of that Navy carrier, I looked up into the sky and saw millions of stars. I was in total awe. It was such a deep experience which I cannot describe in words. It is unimaginable to think that you are that important. How minute you are! Who am I? I am only a speck in the vast universe. I am not that important. My body and its aches are not that important considering the vastness of the universe, and the problems that people face.

Tom once again confirmed for me that perspective is the key to a happier life. If you are having a hard time dealing with life and its challenges, more than likely you are overly focused on your problems. You have placed all your problems into a small ceramic cup, and sitting idly, you are caressing that cup, nostalgically.

I encourage you to transfer the troubles from your ceramic cup to the cosmic container—and watch what happens. While the ceramic cup has only your problems in it, the cosmic container is filled with the problems of the planet. When you compare your problems with all the problems of the world, you are likely to feel grateful and peaceful. You will see your problems with new eyes and face them with renewed strength.

Thank you Tom for being a witness to that truth!

* * *

Ponder and Practice

> Perspective is everything. There is a reason why your eyes are on the top of your body. You are supposed to have a *panoramic vision* not a paranoid look.

> As earthlings, most of our life is centered around earthly stuff. Make it a regular practice to get outside your house into the open fields, and look up into the sky. Make a slow, deliberate, 360 degree turn of your body, and experience the vast universe around, and your place in it.

> Make a list of countries in the world. How many can you come up with, without googling? Expand your *cosmic vision* by learning about other countries and cultures.

23. Dead Man Driving

Jimmy Laduk was a "happy camper" at his assisted living facility where most of his fellow residents were described as "grumpy" and "old." He had little patience for those who longed for the "good old days," or complained about their current life. He was a man in a hurry to enjoy what was left of his life which was in its tenth decade.

Jimmy's body was ninety years old, but his spirit was ageless. Although old age had limited his capacity to walk, Jimmy still had a sharp mind, and was able to engage in meaningful conversations. He had a great sense of humor which made it easy for him to make friends. Jimmy enjoyed driving around the corridors in his motorized scooter which had a fancy license plate which read: *Jimmy's Lexus*. He was a social butter fly who rarely stayed in his room. He would be sitting at the pool chatting, playing cards or enjoying bingo with friends.

Every morning after breakfast, Jimmy drove his *Lexus* to the main lobby to read the news paper. He also stopped at the bulletin board to find out if a resident had passed away. During the past five years, Jimmy had seen death announcements of several of his fellow residents posted on that bulletin board. He used to joke that he checked the board every morning to see if he was dead or alive.

On a Monday morning in February, Jimmy was shocked and amused by the photo he saw on the bulletin board. It was his picture with the caption: "Jimmy Laduk passed away," with the date underneath, and a short bio. He couldn't believe his eyes. For a moment, he thought he was hallucinating. He screamed at the top of his voice, calling the girl at the front desk. When she came, he pointed to the photo on the bulletin board, and the girl was shocked.

She immediately peeled off that photo from the board, and ran towards the office of the nursing director.

When his shock settled, Jimmy chose to see the humor of the episode, and drove around telling residents that he had died and rose again. His family members, however, were not amused. They chastised the management for their carelessness and insensitivity, and for the stress it had caused for all concerned. The management profusely apologized for mistaking him for another Jimmy who had actually died that day.

Two weeks after the incident, Jimmy had a major stroke, and was rushed to the hospital. He died within 48 hours. Jimmy's family members thought that his stroke was precipitated by the incident.

Is it possible that the stroke was the result of a self-fulfilling prophecy? A *self-fulfilling prophecy* is a belief that comes true because we are acting as if it is already true. Although he joked that "the reports of my death has been greatly exaggerated" (*a la* Mark Twain), the reality of seeing his photo on the bulletin board as a dead man, may have hastened his death. No one knows for sure.

But there is a case to be made for the impact of self-fulfilling prophecy in our lives. That may be the reason why nobody really wants to know when and how they are going to die.

Few months ago, there was a Facebook test to find out one's age and cause of death. My curiosity got the best of me, and I did the test. The result: I will die at the age of 95; cause of death: suicide! I was delighted that I had more than three decades left to live, but I was not happy about the cause of death. As the test was not very "life-giving," few hours after posting my results, I deleted it but not soon enough.

A chaplain colleague of mine had seen my post and did the test. He was horrified by the result. He was disturbed and shaken by the cause of death—automobile accident—that he didn't even look at his age at death. As a chaplain who drives around daily to visit his patients, he was afraid and mortified for a few weeks because of the unconscious effect of self-fulfilling prophecy.

Ponder and Practice

> During our waking hours, there is a videotape playing in our heads. Spooling on that tape are about 5000 thoughts a day. Start journaling so that you can sort out your thinking which will bring clarity to your life.

> "The greatest discovery of my generation is that man can change his life simply by changing the attitude of his mind." Let these words of William James help you realize the power of thoughts in your life.

> Monitor your daily thoughts for a week and write them down. After discovering the pattern, discard negative ones and engage only in positive thoughts which could re-wire your brain and re-orient your life.

24. I wish I Could See

Every now and then, I close my eyes and engage in "blindness meditation." I would imagine for a few minutes what it would feel like if I were to go blind. In that split second when my eyelids close, a pall of deep darkness falls over and around me, and I feel a sense of helplessness and paralysis. I can replay on my mental screen, images stored in my memory, but they are nothing like live shots right in front of me. I am paralyzed by the thought of not being able to take a walk in the neighborhood, or to go anywhere by myself, or to drive a car, or to travel to India to see my siblings. Not being able to see the faces of my loved ones, the thought of never being able to read a book or to watch a movie or witness the sunset on the beach, or gaze at the deep ocean or at the stars in the sky makes me shudder with sadness and horror. Life as I know it would be over for me, and the deep sadness welling up in my heart overflows as tears from my closed eyes.

No, no, this is not happening to me, Lord please, give my sight back and I will give half of my wealth to charity, I will forgive everyone and love everybody. I will be a good father, a great husband, a reliable employee, a faithful church member, a productive citizen. I will be super good from this day forward if you please give my sight back because being blind is horrible...I would rather die than be blind.

And then, slowly I open my eyes...it was just a fantasy meditation...I have my sight back...I am relieved, I am joyful, I am thrilled, I am grateful, and I am acutely aware of the gift of sight...and a few days later, I take things for granted again.

Given that you are reading this book means that you have eye sight, and that is reason for celebration. Regardless of what else may be wrong in your life that makes you sad and depressed, if you can see, you should be happy. The eyes are our windows to the world. If those windows are closed, the world as we know it will cease to exist for us.

I had a patient on my hospice team who became blind at the age of 65. She had an active and productive life until blindness set in. She was confined to her room seven days a week, living in total darkness. Morning, noon, and evening didn't mean anything to her; sunny days and rainy nights made no difference. Photo albums in her room collected dust, the TV screen went pitch dark, and she was totally at the mercy of her caregivers.

During every visit, she would say to me with a deep sigh that penetrated the darkness of her room: "I wish I could watch a damn show on this television, I wish I could read a magazine, I wish I could see you!"

If you have eyesight today, don't take it for granted; smile, be happy, be grateful, jump up and down, appreciate it, and celebrate it.

* * *

Ponder and Practice

> The human eye is amazing and miraculous. Each eye contains some 130 million photo-receptors that translate light into nerve impulses which travel along the optic nerves to the brain, where the rays are assembled into a coherent picture...wow...If you have eyesight, jump up and down and praise God.

> Most of the time, on most days, we are merely looking not really *seeing*. Change the way you look at the world from being a *passing glance* to a *passionate gaze*. Practice this by deliberately making eye contact with people, and looking into their eyes while talking and listening to them.

> Periodically engage in blindness meditation. Imagine that you are blind for a day. Think about all the implications of that situation.

67

25. Death Denial

Death is a taboo topic among humans. The denial and discomfort about this dreaded topic is beautifully and humorously depicted in the recently released book, *Can't We Talk About Something More Pleasant: A memoir* by Ros Chast, staff cartoonist for *The New Yorker*.

In my line of work as a hospice chaplain, I find that a lot of patients with terminal diagnosis, are afraid or reluctant to talk about the **D** word. Once, the daughter of a patient prohibited me from identifying myself as the hospice chaplain because that would scare her dad. She advised that I remove my hospice badge, and identify myself as a representative from a *Life-insurance company*. I have a hard time pretending to be an insurance agent, but I did it anyway to gain access to the patient with the hope that I could help prepare the patient and the family for the inevitable.

Life Insurance agents are very clever. They will sell you a policy without mentioning the **D** word. One expression they use is: *If something happens to you...your family will be protected.* Are you kidding me? Of course *something* happens to me every day. I get caught up in traffic, I forget to charge my cell phone, or a friend calls with a bad news. But that is not what they mean. They mean *death*, but they won't say the word.

Another expression is: *In the unlikely event of something happening to you.* It sounds like an announcement from pilots at the beginning of a flight. *In the unlikely event of a water landing, the cushions under the seat will inflate.* A plane landing on water is an unlikely event, death is not.

Another tactic they use to get around the **D** word goes something like this: *In the event of your premature passing, your family will be protected.*

Premature? The word implies that we are supposed to live to a certain age. It implies that a certain number of years are guaranteed and if we die before that, it is considered premature. That is only in our mind. Unlike automobiles and appliances, we don't come with warranty papers in our back pocket. In fact, we arrive naked, with no pockets and no warranties. When it comes to death, there are no guarantees. It could happen to anybody, anywhere, at any age, at any time.

We started dying the day we were formed in our mother's womb. It is a miracle that we go on living year after year, in the midst of so many life threatening events and situations.

Death denial is actually not healthy. As each day passes, we are 24 hours closer to the edge of the grave or the mouth of the urn. Denying that reality and pretending to ignore it is an exercise in extreme futility. By refusing to acknowledge the impermanence of our existence, we are writing our own script for an anxious and lethargic life.

The more we think about death, the more fully we live. That may sound counter intuitive, but that is the truth. According to Mother Theresa, *People who are unable to confront the fact of their own mortality are unable to fully appreciate life.*

Bishop John Shelby Spong recommends that "human beings must dance with death before they will ever be able to rejoice in life or laugh with it." He says that he "lives in the appreciation that it is the presence of death that actually makes my life precious, since it calls me to live each day fully, and it is by living fully that I enter the timelessness of life."

In ancient Rome, when a general took a victory parade through the streets, legend has it that he was trailed by a servant whose job it was to repeat to him *Memento Mori (Remember, you will die)*. We may not be able to hire a servant to remind us but we should be aware of this reality on a daily basis, not to be obsessed with it, but like a glance in a rear view mirror.

Denying death is not going to make it disappear. We should talk about it openly, prepare for it in advance and, face it squarely. I believe that unless and until we acknowledge and accept the mystery of death, we will not be able to understand or celebrate the miracle of life and live fully.

69

Ponder and Practice

> Once, somebody wondered as to how I deal with dying people daily in my job as a hospice chaplain. I told him that he too is working with dying people every day. All of us live with, work with, drive with, shop with, and do everything else with *dying people* all day, every day, all the time.

> Do a "death meditation." Lie down comfortably, close your eyes and imagine you have only 30 days left on this earth. Explore your thoughts and feelings about that news, and the behaviors you will engage in for the next 30 days.

> Visit a local cemetery, walk around the graves, and imagine being in the grave.

26. 65 is the new 45

Cleo is 90 years old. Her aging body needs a wheelchair for transport but her mind is still sharp. Even though she was a young widow at age 55, Cleo didn't remarry as she had "very bad experiences with men." She was born and raised Methodist and "dabbled in Catholicism for a while," but she is not a "fan of religion" now. "I am not into holy-roly rituals," she says.

She is happy to talk to me but refuses my offer to pray with her. "God hasn't done much for me in 90 years; do you think your prayer at this stage of the game is going to make any difference?" As much as I appreciated her straight-shooting and filter-free talk, I was surprised by her non-nonchalant approach to life and death at her age.

Cleo knows what hospice means and she has neither any fear of dying nor any hope of after-life. "I will go six feet under and that is it; end of story," she said.

My visit began with a question: "So, how are you today?"

Cleo: "I am waiting to die."

Me: "What do you mean? Tell me more."

Cleo: "What is there to tell. I have nobody to live for and nothing to look forward to. My husband died years ago. I have no children or grandchildren. All my friends are gone. An attorney is taking care of my affairs. All I have is this dog—pointing to her puppy—and this is no way to live, peeing in diapers, pooping in clothes, and eating pureed food."

I was lost for words.

Cleo took advantage of my silence and asked me, "So how old are you?"

Me: "I am sixty five."

Cleo: *"You don't have a long way to go!"*

Cleo's comment hit me hard. The prospect of her current plight, becoming my not-so-distant plight, gave me a quick quiver. It is a disheartening thought, an utterly unappealing prospect. Having served hundreds of patients with Cleo's profile in several assisted living facilities over the years, the very thought of living in one makes me sick. I hope and pray that my life never comes to that.

There are no guarantees. I have no idea how it is all going to shake out. That is why my upcoming milestone birthday is causing me some unexpected mental dissonance that I am embarrassed to admit. I am surprised that despite my above average awareness about the mystery of life, I am not ready to be sixty five years old. In olden times, it was considered old.

Cleo was right. *I don't have a long way to go!*

Therefore, it will be disingenuous on my part to say that I am looking forward to my 65th birth day in a month. The only silver lining at the start of the silver phase of my life is that I qualify for *Medicare,* and that I don't have to deal with the largely lugubrious and onerous private health insurance system. Perks like senior discount at movie theaters, and the senior omelet at Denny's restaurants are appetizing. Also the likelihood of being kidnapped for ransom is significantly reduced. Other than that, it is downhill, for the most part.

You don't have a long way to go—I don't take Cleo's comment as a prediction of my imminent demise. Nevertheless, it is one more reminder of my personal mortality.

As a hospice chaplain, I have witnessed hundreds of deaths. Death and dying are part of my everyday vocabulary. Funerals and memorials are part and parcel of my professional life. And yet—all things being equal—knowing that I may have about twenty years to live on this planet is not a palatable thought.

It is unnerving to think that the streets and buildings in my neighborhood will outlive me. I am envious of young people who have more than half a century left on their life-tab. I am jealous of my son who is only twenty, and has forty five years to catch up with where I am today, and then some. It is a "holy jealousy," but jealousy nonetheless!

I know these are irrational thoughts. They jump around in my monkey-mind as clowns in a circus tent. I know it is for the purpose of entertainment only.

I am okay with being sixty-five. In fact, I am going to affirm daily: *Sixty-five is the new forty-five!*

* * *

Ponder and Practice

> Write down your name and age on a piece of paper. Look at it closely. Are you comfortable with your current age? Do you engage in any age-hiding techniques?

> Do an "old-age meditation." Imagine you are 90 years old. You can barely see, hardly hear, appetite is poor, taste is lost. You are wearing a diaper and confined to a wheelchair. Write down your thoughts and feelings.

> Eat right, sleep well, exercise 30 minutes a day, meditate 30 minutes a day, watch less TV and more TED talks, read books, have an open mind, be flexible, erase absolutes, embrace relativity, raise your offense-level, love everyone, and feel 20 years younger than your chronological age!

27. Priscilla's Fears

I don't want to be cremated because I am terrified of fire, said Priscila. The story behind her fear of fire is that her childhood home in Michigan was burned down more than fifty years ago. She barely escaped with second degree burns, while her little brother, who was asleep at the time, died in that fatal fire. Although her bodily scars have disappeared over time, her psychological scars remain which explains her fears about cremation.

Burial underground also was unacceptable for Priscilla; she did not want to be "suffocated" in the grave.

What about burial at sea, I asked and she quipped: "I don't know how to swim."

Priscilla was a nervous patient. She had this flair for irrationality, not uncommon among people, when it comes to death and dying. I had a patient who was afraid to sleep at night because he thought that most people died in their sleep. So he would drink plenty of coffee and spend all night watching television and sleep during the day. Ironically, he died in sleep during the day.

"Is there any other method of body disposal, less scary than cremation and burial?" Priscilla asked.

The only one I could think of was the way the Parsis disposed of their bodies in India. The Parsis, who came to India from Persia (Iran) a thousand years ago with their *Zoroastrian* faith, have gone to great lengths to maintain their unique funeral rituals. The Parsi corpse is exposed to the rays of the sun, while the corpse is consumed or devoured by birds of prey — vultures and crows.

For *Zoroastrians*, burying or cremating the dead is seen as polluting nature. So for centuries, the Parsis in Mumbai have relied on vultures to do the work.

The Parsi temple and place of disposal of the dead is often referred to as the *Tower of Silence*. One of the most famous Towers of Silence is in Mumbai. Most of these towers of silence are vast open spaces with a temple at the entrance. The vast open spaces are home to vultures that eat the flesh of the dead.

The *Tower of Silence* will have a perimeter wall which encloses the place where the bodies are kept. Inside, there are three concentric circles. The bodies of the men are arranged on the outer circle and the women in the middle circle and children are placed in the innermost circle. Nobody is allowed to enter the sacred burial place, except the pall bearers.

The principle behind offering the dead body to nature and birds is supposed to be the last act of charity of a Parsi, wherein he donates his body to birds for food. The body of the dead Parsi is brought in a coffin to the *Tower of Silence*, and after a ceremony, it is taken inside by special pall bearers. The body is then left in the open. Nobody can visit the body again once it is committed to the *Tower of Silence*.

Conversion to Zorastrian religion and moving to India were not options for Priscilla. Nor was she going to be convinced by my rational arguments against the myths and misunderstandings about death and body disposal. So I told her a story.

On a Friday morning at 6 a.m., I arrived at the local surgical center for my colonoscopy. After completing the paperwork, I was prepped for the procedure. The anesthesiologist and the doctor showed up at 7 a.m. and they explained the procedure. I remember the anesthesiologist poking my arm and asking me to count, and barely before I was able to reach five, I was fully asleep.

Are you okay, Mr. Paul? were the words I heard as I tried to open my groggy eyes. By this time, I was in a different room and the time was 10 a.m. I had absolutely no awareness of the previous three hours or of the medical procedure that I went through. There were at least three professionals around me, and plenty of probing, prodding, and poking going on, in the most sensitive areas of my body. I was totally unaware because I was under anesthesia.

Death is like a profound, prolonged, permanent anesthesia, I told Priscilla.

She fell silent for a moment. Her fear of fire, earth and water may not have been abated—but I was elated that Priscilla offered me an opportunity to share an experience that has helped me to deal with my death-related anxieties.

* * *

Ponder and Practice

> Are you afraid to die? Is it a fear of the death-experience itself or is it a fear of dying before doing anything meaningful with your life?

> How would you like to be dispatched: Burial in the ground, burial at sea, or cremation? Think about the pros and cons of each, and make a choice that fits your needs and desires, and those of your loved ones.

> Consider organ donation and/or whole body donation and give the gift of life even in death. Check out these websites and register as a donor. *www.organdonor.gov www.Sciencecare.com*

28. Lexus and Cadillac

As I exited the elevator to the third floor of the assisted living facility, my heart took a few extra beats. I was going to visit a family that was described by other team members as demanding services beyond the scope of our practice, delusional about the nature of hospice care, and in denial about the patient's prognosis.

I took a few deep breaths and knocked on the door. Inside the apartment there was an L-shaped leather sofa and two separate recliners. The patient, Mr. Norm was resting on the sofa with his wife Edna, sitting next to him. Their two daughters, Rhoda and Randi, who live out of state, had flown in, to help their parents "situate" themselves after their dad had been admitted to hospice care.

Norm owned a clothing store in New York where he and his wife worked hard and made it into a successful business. They raised four children, two sons and two daughters, who have become successful in their own right. Two of their grandchildren are medical doctors, and one granddaughter is an attorney. Norm and Edna had rightfully earned their bragging rights for a family that diligently followed the script to realize the "American dream." At their ripe age of 92 and 90, they should be happy, relaxed, content, and peaceful.

They were anything but!

I knew I had to tread gingerly and speak gently because my social worker had warned me that the patient is very sensitive and the daughters are very protective of their parents. The daughters did not want us to use the word "hospice" around their parents. They were wary of anybody who might say or do anything to puncture the emotional veil they had placed around their elderly parents. So I made a decision to listen more and speak less.

Although Norm was 92, he looked no older than 75 because of his smooth skin and ability to communicate. He was recovering from a recent bout with pneumonia and had lingering breathing issues. He was incredulous that he was incapable of doing the things he used to do, such as walking, cooking, driving, and swimming.

During my entire life, I was never sick. I don't ever remember having even a headache. I have never taken any medication. I was always healthy and did everything I wanted to do. Now this? I can't get up without somebody helping me, I can't walk even to the bathroom; I need this damn oxygen tube hanging from the nose, and I can't go anywhere without dragging that damn oxygen tank. This sucks...

His wife and daughters joined Norm in his chorus of complaints.

My instinctive reaction was to slap him and bring him back to consciousness about the utter lack of gratitude for the amazing life he has had, and to point out the inevitable indignities of growing old. As a professional, however, I am aware that I cannot react mindlessly, and that I should respond mindfully.

In my fifteen years as a hospice chaplain, I have visited hundreds of patients. Norm belongs in the top one percent of individuals who has had an "amazing run" through this race called life. For him, almost everything went right. He had a happy and stable marriage for 67 years. I noticed that his affection for his wife had not diminished over the years. They genuinely seemed to cherish each other's company, after all these years. They often exchanged knowing winks and squeezed each other's hands during my visit. Norm's fear was that Edna would be helpless without him. Edna's anxiety was Norm won't be around to take care of her.

Ninety two years "without even a headache and no medications" is an enviable achievement in physical health. Lesser mortals would have "kicked the bucket" before reaching that age. Had they lived, they would have gone through a long list of ailments including arthritis, Alzheimer's, and a series of surgeries.

For Norm, his 92 years of perfect health should have been a huge reason for grateful celebration, but it was not. He was griping about the inevitable ailments of old age with no apparent awareness about the impermanence of life.

So chaplain, you are the man with answers. Tell me, why is this happening to me?

I have always believed in telling the truth in love. Besides, I didn't want to perpetuate the unrealistic expectation that he was going to recover from his age-related decline, and restored back to perfect health. I didn't want to throw a rope into the deep sea of denial where he was merely treading water.

So, I asked Norm if he wanted the short answer or the long answer. *I am 92 and I don't think I have enough time left for the long answer; so give me the short answer,* he replied.

"It is your age, Norm," I said.

"What you mean?"

He had an incredulous look in his eyes.

"A 92 year old body does not bounce back like a 19 year old body. It is as simple as that." I said.

At this point, I had earned enough trust to speak to him in clear terms. So I told him about my Lexus.

When I came out of the Lexus dealership in Margate, Florida, I was in the driver's seat of a brand new Lexus ES 300. The year was 2000. That shiny maroon colored car had just 13 miles on the odometer, an exquisite interior, and an elegant exterior. The leather seats were spotless. The engine worked perfectly. After being on the road for 13 years, the leather faded, the paint chipped, the pipes rusted, had several dents, and there was even a big gash on one side caused by my lawn mower. When the transmission began to fail, I finally traded it in for another car. My favorite Lexus had 164,308 miles. It was on its way to the auction block.

"Our bodies are very much like a car," I told Norm. It is a miracle that it works the way it does for so many years, considering what we do to it, with it, and what we put into it.

Norm seemed to like my story because he told me about the beat-up Cadillac he inherited from his father.

Two months after my visit, Norm died. When I visited Edna for bereavement support, she told me that after my visit, her husband used to refer to his body as a "used car ready for the junkyard."

Ponder and Practice

> Norm was oblivious about his obsolescence. Read this awesome book, *Being Mortal*, by Atul Gawande. Not much of a reader? Watch on YouTube, *Being Mortal: Medicine and What Matters in the End.*

> Norm's daughters were shielding him from "bad news." I think they were underestimating his ability to cope. He probably has faced more hardships before they were even born! Don't treat the elderly like little children.

> Select two photos from your album: a baby picture and your current photo. Study them closely and write down your feelings.

29. Dying Daily

When I tell people that I am a hospice chaplain, the usual reactions are: *"That must be depressing," "seeing death every day must be stressful," "being near dead bodies must be scary."* The conversation abruptly ends because nobody wants to dwell in a dull, deadly domain. One day a guy said to me in a smart-aleck way: *"So, you work with dying people?"* And tongue in cheek, I responded: *"You work with dying people too; the difference is, I am aware of it and you are not."*

We all live, work, commute, worship, and do everything else with dying people. We are all dying each day.

Death was dreadful, depressing, scary, and dreary, until I understood the real meaning of death a few years ago. Since then, I have been able to accept it, be comfortable with it, and even embrace it.

My first breakthrough came about twelve years ago when I observed the dying process in one of my patients. Jane was 74 and she had lung cancer. On the day she died, I sat at her bedside, and I began to observe her breathing pattern. It became farther and farther apart, until she took her *last breath*. With that last breath, everything that was Jane ended, only to leave behind a lifeless shell of a body. Jane was her breaths; her 74 years of life was lived, celebrated, and accomplished in those breaths.

As I watched Jane take her last breath, I was reminded of the creation story in the book of *Genesis* where it says that after forming the first human from the clay of the earth, *God blew into his nostrils the **breath of life** and so man became a living being.* Even though I don't take that story literally, the idea that *human life is the breath of God,* is striking. Every human being breathes the same way, regardless of where s/he lives. And breath is with us from the moment we are born until the moment we die.

For me, breath is the best proof, *under my very nose*, that God exists. I live, move, and have my being in God. And since death is nothing but the merging of my last breath into the Eternal Breath of God, there is nothing to fear.

Moments after Jane died, it seemed as if her facial skin was tightening and her face became smoother. I noticed a *glow* on her face which seemed like the *blush* caused by God's welcoming kiss at the gate of heaven.

So for me, death as *return to the Source* is comforting while death as *end* is scary.

Since I started working in hospice, my life has become much more peaceful and joyful. I am no longer stressed out or worried as I once was. It has become easy to love everybody. I have learned to live more in the *now* because I am constantly reminded that tomorrow is not guaranteed. As I witness death on a daily basis, I am acutely aware that all I have is this moment, today. It helps me unwind the complex knots of my adult mind, and become like a child who only thinks about how things *are* right now, unlike the adult who is able to think about how things *were* in the past or *should be* in the future.

During our adulthood, we learn about *later* and get stuck there without the ability to return to and live in the *now*. Death awareness clearly helps me to be "in the moment" and enjoy the now. Awareness of death gives perspective on every aspect of life. It keeps me grounded and helps me to focus on the essentials of life.

Death awareness is the best antidote for anxiety and depression. Depression is about the past; anxiety is about the future. Death awareness mitigates the tyranny of both and keeps me in the present.

* * *

Ponder and Practice

> Write down your date of birth on a piece of paper. Then write down the same date a year prior to that date. For example if you were born on July 1, 1955, where were you on July 1, 1954? Ponder that!

> Everyone breathes air wherever they are; everyone breathes the same way whoever they are; everyone stops breathing when they die. There is no Christian breathing, or a Muslim breathing or a Hindu breathing. Is it possible that our bi-racial, bi-partisan breathing could breach the gap, and bind us together as one human family?

> Read Eckhart Tolle's book: *The Power of Now*. You will breathe better and become a beautiful being.

30. Die *Before* You Die

An idea that has helped me become comfortable with death and dying is Eckhart Tolle's advice: *Die before you die and find out there is no death.* That profound statement needs explanation.

When we face death, all those things we normally consider to be important become unimportant and irrelevant: our name, status, position, possessions, money, job, car, house, etc. Things that we usually fight for and become upset about if lost, turn out to be insignificant. At our deathbed, the whole idea of ownership peels like an onion, and reveals itself as totally meaningless. The tragedy is that, what we are really looking for—peace, love, and joy—have already been with us and within us yet largely obscured by wrongly identifying with things outside of us.

I have seen people dying with millions of dollars in their brokerage accounts, precious jewelry in their safety deposit boxes, cherished paintings on their living room walls, and designer clothes in their closets. Things that they were so attached to, worried about losing, and were reluctant to share, had to be left behind.

I remember the death of my neighbor, Jim, who was very fond of his house. He meticulously took care of it, both inside and outside. If somebody parked a car in front of his house, and a tire happened to be on the grass, Jim would hunt down the driver of that car and insist that he move it. He got upset with kids in the neighborhood who would run through his backyard, and might step on the sprinkler heads and damage them. Jim had several things in the house that he cherished. He had a motor cycle he worshiped. Every Saturday, he cleaned and polished it, and every Sunday he went riding with his buddies.

Jim was diagnosed with lung cancer at the young age of 53. After being on hospice care for six months, he died.

I vividly remember the scene when the undertaker placed Jim's body in a plastic bag, covered it with a green blanket, placed it on a gurney, rolled it to the curb, pushed it into the back of his white van, and drove away in the middle of the night. The flickering tail lights of that white van still flash in my mind.

It was an eerie sight. The man who was the owner of his house, and the head of his household, left in the middle of the night, alone and empty handed, never to return again. He had to leave his house and everything in and around it, behind. No U-haul was hooked up to the van that carried his remains.

So, if we can live our lives, as if the external, material things are unimportant, without enormous attachments to stuff and people, thus *die to the world, and die to the self,* then at the time of physical death, we will find out that death is not scary at all, because *we have already died to everything that makes death scary.*

In fact, facing one's own death directly can empower us to live our lives more fully, and thus thrive in life.

* * *

Ponder and Practice

> Think of a phrase you want to have on your tombstone. Write it down. What does it mean?

> The Master once told of a man in the countryside who had an obsession with acquiring land. "I wish I had more land," he said one day. "But why" asked the Master. "Don't you have enough already?"

"If I had more land, I could raise more cows."

"And what would you do with them?"

"Sell them and make money."

"For what?"

"To buy more land and raise a lot of cows..."

~ Anthony De Mello

> Leave a little space around your attachments. It will serve as a buffer zone to soften the shock of your separations.

31. Death is Beautiful

Beautiful is not the adjective that we usually use to describe death. Words like "terrible," "horrible," "painful," "tragic," and "unfortunate," seem more appropriate. The word beautiful and death are like oil and water in the minds of many.

After working as a hospice chaplain for many years, and having witnessed the death of hundreds of patients, I like to affirm that the death experience is beautiful—for the dying person. Of course, for the bereaved, it is tragic and painful and horrible, especially if the death is that of a young person or unexpected and untimely.

There are several other factors that can make death a really horrible experience for the living. In fact, there is no good time to die because our human tendency is to hold on to life forever, if we can.

To make sense of this unavoidable life event, I like to see it as the most beautiful experience in life.

Death is like going home which is a joyful experience for most people. I remember flying home to India to visit my parents and siblings. Even though it is a long and tiring trip of about 32 hours—three flights through three different time zones, and two sleepless nights, not to mention the horrible jet lag—when that plane approaches my home town airport, I am happy and delighted because soon I will be with my loved ones.

It is morning when I arrive home, and mom has prepared a sumptuous Indian breakfast with all my favorite dishes. I will sit down and enjoy that delicious meal, being surrounded by my parents and siblings who are gazing at me because they haven't seen me in two years. That meal has the feel of the much anticipated feast in the Heavenly Kingdom. Even though I am physically tired, I am delighted and joyful to be surrounded by pure love. I have the same experience of exhilaration and joy when returning to the USA., because Judy and the boys will be waiting for me at the airport at this end.

Multiply the anticipation and joy of going to your earthly home by a million times, and that will be the joy of returning to your original home, which is the heart of God.

Before we were tenants in the womb of our mothers, we were residents in the heart of God.

Death is the biggest mystery of life. Nobody knows exactly what happens at the moment of death. Near Death Experience (NDE) studies have described death *as the most beautiful human experience.* It must be, and that is why nobody who has died has ever come back to this world filled with pain and suffering.

In his book, *Home with God in a Life that Never Ends*, Neale Donald Walsch describes death as "experiencing complete oneness with God." There are no words to adequately describe this feeling, partly because the feeling is huge. This is how he describes what happens at the moment of death:

It might be characterized as a single, enormous, conglomerate of feelings that encompasses a thousand individual feelings, now slowly filling the soul. A feeble attempt to describe it would call it the feeling of being warmly embraced, deeply comforted, dearly cherished, profoundly appreciated, genuinely treasured, softly nurtured, profoundly understood, completely forgiven, wholly absolved, long awaited, happily welcome, totally honored, joyously celebrated, absolutely protected, instantly perfected, and unconditionally loved—all at once.

Reports of the last words of Steve Jobs before his death seem to shed light on the notion of death as the most beautiful human experience. According to his sister, Mona Simpson, after making it through one final night, her brother began to slip away.

"But with that will, that work ethic, that strength, there was also sweet Steve's capacity for wonderment, the artist's belief in the ideal, the still more beautiful later."

"Steve's final words were: *"Oh wow. Oh wow. Oh wow."*

His neurons must have been misfiring at the final moments; or he must have been delusional.

Or is it possible that, this creative genius who invented the magically awesome iPhone was beholding something more magical, mysterious, miraculous, and momentous?

Was he experiencing what *no eye has seen, no ear has heard, and no mind has imagined—the things that God has prepared for those who love him?* (1Corinthians 1:29)

* * *

Ponder and Practice

> Before we were tenants in our mother's womb, we were residents in the heart of God. When we die, we melt back into the heart of God.

> You can make your death beautiful by making your life beautiful. Are you experiencing a beautiful life now? If not, think of five things you can do to make it beautiful.

> Do you want to make your death a beautiful experience for your loved ones? If so, fill out and sign the document called *The Five Wishes.* Your loved ones will thank you forever! Available at: ***www.agingwithdignity.org***

32. Endings *are* Beginnings

One day I was visiting a patient, Robert, who was 87. As he lay motionless, his wife Mary sat near his bed, tearfully anxious and refusing to let go of the "love of my life." They were married for nearly sixty years. The thought of living her life without Robert was unthinkable for Mary.

"He was the man of the house and he did everything around. I don't know what bills to pay or how to pay them. I don't know how to drive or put gas in the car. He did all that." Mary's anxiety was palpable; her fears were real. There is no easy solution to the problems Mary will face after her husband dies.

Mary looked into my eyes and said: "You are a man of God, tell me why people have to die; and don't just quote verses from the Bible." I was humbled by the question but stumped by the directive not to quote from the Bible. I was trained to use the Bible as the *go to book* in situations like these.

I said a short prayer in my heart asking God for the right words to calm Mary's fears. My attention was drawn to a playpen in the middle of the living room. In that playpen was a beautiful baby, laughing and playing with his toys. He was full of life and joy. Mary pointed to the baby and said: "He is the only thing that keeps me going." The baby in the playpen was her great-grand son named Robert, who was called *Bobby.* It was no coincidence that her husband's name was also Robert.

In the bedroom was Robert I, her husband, who had lived a full life and was preparing to *go home.* In the playpen was Robert III, her great-grandson, barely beginning his life. I pointed out to Mary the irony and mystery of the cycle of life. I made her aware that all experiences in life are *by contrast.* Love and hate, joy and sorrow, night and day, up and down, birth and death are all experienced in pairs. There is no rainbow without the rain. We cannot have one without the other. Unless one knows both, one knows neither.

As the Indian Guru, Sri N. Maharaj says, *between the banks of pain and pleasure, the river of life flows. It is only when the mind refuses to flow with life and gets stuck at the banks that it becomes a problem.*

I gave Mary a copy of the poem *On Dying* which was given to me by a grieving widow.

I am standing on the sea shore,

A ship spreads her white sails and starts for the ocean;

I stand watching her until she fades on the horizon.

Someone at my side says "she's gone."

Just at that moment when someone says "she's gone,"

There are others who are watching her coming and saying: "here she comes!"

All endings are also beginnings. If we can make that phrase part of our conscious awareness, we will thrive even in the midst of painful loss.

Even though Mary had told me not to quote the Bible, I go to Jesus first when I grapple with life's major dilemmas. His comforting words in this context are: "Unless a grain of wheat falls to the ground and dies, it remains just a grain of wheat; but if it dies, it produces much fruit." (John 12:24)

There are no better words to explain the mystery of death and the miracle of life.

* * *

Ponder and Practice

> Watch this incredible video on You tube. *The Fall of Freddie the Leaf,* by Leo Buscaglia. This ten minute video could change your ideas about life and death.

> Take a stroll through a forest or a park. Focus your attention on a particular tree, carefully study its leaves, their size, shape, texture, color etc. *See* them falling to the ground to make room for new leaves! Observe that no tree stubbornly holds on to its leaves, but let them fall off freely, surrendering to nature's rhythm.

> In our binary thinking, we say, black & white, up & down, night & day, good & bad, etc. So, what is the opposite of life? Life&...? If you answered, "death," you are wrong!

33. Write Your Obituary

I had a friend who was just 51 when she was diagnosed with ovarian cancer. She was a nurse on my hospice team. When she realized that she would not survive her cancer, she ordered a license plate with the word OVARY to raise awareness about ovarian cancer. Two months after the diagnosis, she went to the funeral home to select a mausoleum. She wanted to be on the top draw on the wall in the mausoleum. She discussed with her family the kind of funeral service she wanted: the hymns, the readings, the readers, the pall bearers, and the venue for the reception. She also wrote her own obituary. All that her daughter had to do was to fill in the date of death and send it to the local paper.

Writing one's own obituary may sound morose at first, but it can be a liberating and transforming experience. It gives you an opportunity to spell out who you are, what you believe, and to examine your life-journey. Reading your own obituary could be a life changing experience.

The experience of Alfred Nobel, inventor of dynamite, who later established the *Nobel Prize for Peace*, is a case in point. About 130 years ago, Alfred Nobel picked up the morning paper, and to his horror, read his own obituary in that paper. His brother had died, but apparently a newspaper writer mistakenly believed that Alfred had passed away. The obituary stated, *The merchant of death is dead. Dr. Alfred Nobel, who became rich by finding ways to kill more people faster than ever before, died yesterday.*

Nobel was reportedly forced to re-think his life when he read his own obituary. He was disturbed by the distressing assessment of his life and decided to leave a more honorable legacy. Before his death, he signed over most of his estate to the establishment of the Nobel Peace Prize and achievements in the fields of literature, economics, medicine and the sciences. A man who amassed his fortune by producing explosives became an apostle of peace.

What if we had an opportunity to read our own obituary? I think it would help us to honestly evaluate our lives, declare our loyalties, and sort out our priorities. It helped me after I wrote my own obituary a few years ago, as part of an exercise in a men's group. It was a scary and freeing experience.

After I wrote the year of my birth and drew the dash, I found it very hard to write the year of my death. I put 2035, hoping that I will live to see my 85th birthday. It is actually 4.5 years more than my life expectancy estimated by insurance agents. It will be 15 bonus years from a biblically perfect life of *three scores and ten* and I would be very happy if I reach that age. However, if I lose my mental capacity to process life, and if I were to enter a vegetative state where my existence will be prolonged with pills and pipes, thus becoming a burden to others, my family should have no qualms about expediting my expiration and let me go in peace. I will have no problem exiting this physical plane of existence at an earlier date.

The first sentence of my obituary was the hardest to write. *Paul Veliyathil transitioned from this life to the next...*and then I stopped. I could not write for a long time. The very thought of dying, leaving all the familiar things, and especially leaving Judy, Johnny, and Tommy, brought torrents of tears. Every time I see a dead body in a coffin, a fleeting thought that I will have to take my place in that box one day, occurs to me ever so briefly. But I dismiss it as something that will happen in a distant future.

But even in a distant future, it is an unacceptable prospect, an unpalatable thought. But I am keenly aware of the fact that the inevitable will happen, that death will knock on my door, that my eyes will be closed for ever, that my body will be burned in 2000 degree Fahrenheit, and that I will be reduced to two or three pounds of grainy ashes. That awareness makes this moment valuable: today's life precious, everyone around me lovable, and life the ultimate gift.

In my obituary, I did not use the word *died,* which sounds like a dead word (pun intended). I did not want to say *passed away,*

94

which seems to be a term reserved for the death of famous people. In fact, *passed on* is a more accurate expression, because *passed away* indicates going to a place far away.

Passed on means, transcending to a new location. I did not want to say *expired* as it sounds like the expiration of a magazine subscription. The word *departed* was unacceptable as it implies traveling to some other place. *Kicked the bucket* was ruled out as too crass. I believe that the word *transition* best describes the death experience as entering a new phase of life—in a new dimension, the spiritual dimension. For those who live in that dimension now, death should be an easy transition.

* * *

Ponder and Practice

> Pick up a newspaper today and read all the obituaries. Which one impressed you the most and why?

> Why do you think obituaries usually focus on the material accomplishments of the deceased?

> Write your obituary. If you were to give an imaginary title for that, what would that be, and why?

34. Exit Strategy

I entered this world on October 6, 1950. I just showed up in a village called Muttuchira, in southern India. I had no choice in the matter. I did not choose my parents or my siblings or the order of birth as a middle child who apparently gets no attention. I did not choose the country of my birth. I had absolutely no say or vote in anything concerning my beginnings. But as far as my endings, I have some choices. We all have choices. Not to make them would be foolish and foolhardy.

No one goes on a journey without making advance preparations. Booking a ticket, reserving a hotel, and renting a car are normal steps we take before embarking on a journey. If it is an international trip, we also have to have documents, like a passport and visas. It is mind boggling that most people make no preparation for the final and ultimate journey of their lives. Failing to make pre-arrangements can cause plenty of heartache and frustration for your surviving loved ones.

One of the goals of hospice care is to prepare patients for a peaceful death, and making funeral arrangements prior to death is part of that process. Just like the **D** word, it is very hard for some people to say the **F** word, I mean the word *funeral*. I have encountered many people who superstitiously think that if they make pre-arrangements, it will hasten their death.

Let me tell you the story of Mike, who unexpectedly died in the hospital at 8 p.m. on a Sunday night. Although he was 87, neither Mike nor his family ever talked about death or made any prior arrangements. His daughter Lisa said: "It was kind of unexpected; he was fine the day before; we were kind of caught off guard." These are statements no intelligent human should ever make when it comes to death and dying, especially about someone who is in his eighties and on hospice care.

Since there were no pre-arrangements, the hospital gave Lisa the name of a franchise funeral home in the city and the body was taken there. The next morning, Lisa called the funeral home to discuss the funeral plans. She was told that she had to make an appointment with the funeral director. The funeral director, of course, wants to sell a few accessories to Lisa which would cost her thousands of dollars. I don't blame the funeral director for wanting to make extra money, and I have little sympathy for Lisa who has to part with her money due to her negligence or that of her father.

Lisa was angry and frustrated that she had to come in person to meet the funeral director who could only meet with her at 3 p.m., because he was busy with two other funerals that day. This is what happens when we wait till the last minute, because others' schedules won't coincide with our needs. Lisa was so outraged, and so she called a friend who suggested a different funeral home. Her father's body was picked up from the first funeral home, and was taken to the second funeral home.

Such post-death frustrations and indignities could have been avoided, had there been some forethought and planning about the kind of exit Mike wanted from this world.

* * *

Ponder and Practice

> Are you happy with the place of your birth and the country of your origin? If you could trade those, what would you choose?

> Do you have an exit strategy? If not, start the process today!

> If you are thinking about a funeral, make sure you compare the "Funeral Pricing Checklist" of at least three funeral homes. Check out this website: *www.consumer.ftc.gov*

35. Use the "F" Word

There was a daughter of a hospice patient who refused to discuss the topic of death or make funeral arrangements. She got upset with me for broaching the topic of funeral because "I don't want to even think about it now; it is very upsetting." Her false thinking, *if I don't make arrangements, my mother won't die*, didn't work. Her mother died at 5 p.m. on a Monday in August. I was called to the house to comfort the family, and to help with the transferring of the body from the house to the funeral home. When I arrived, there were about 15 people milling around the house, but the daughter was nowhere to be found.

When I asked where Patricia was, her husband said: "Oh, she went to the funeral home." When her mother died, Patricia had called the funeral home but the phone was busy, so she got into her car and drove there. Imagine that drive in heavy traffic to make funeral arrangements! She began driving with a heart filled with sorrow and tears running down her cheek, leaving the lifeless body of her mother in the house.

While Patricia was away making arrangements for the removal of her mother's body, a cousin of hers showed up. She called a friend of hers who was a funeral director and made arrangements without consulting Patricia. She thought she was being helpful. The problem was that undertakers from two funeral homes showed up at the same time. After some negotiations, Patricia allowed the body of her mother to be removed by the funeral home that had quoted $500 less for the service!

When your loved one dies, it is the time to grieve, not the time to make arrangements or negotiate price so that you can give the remains to the lowest bidder.

Let us face it, the funeral industry is a business. When you go to a funeral home, of course there is sympathy and compassion, but they are also talking dollars and cents; a lot of dollars.

The other day I met a family who paid $13,000 for a funeral at a local cemetery. It was a last minute arrangement. Had they made pre-need arrangements, they could have saved thousands of dollars.

When you make funeral arrangements *after* the loved one dies, you are sitting in front of a funeral director with a grieving heart and a foggy brain. When you are grieving deeply, you are not thinking clearly. You don't have the luxury of time to consider the *pros* and *cons* of the options the funeral director is offering. Under the emotional fog of loss and grief, you sign up for unnecessary services at inflated costs.

We should get off the high horse of death-denial, and walk on the flat ground of reality, and make pre-arrangements for our exit when our minds are clear and our emotions are under control. It could save a lot of grief and plenty of green.

* * *

Ponder and Practice

> The cremation rate in the United States has been increasing steadily from 3.56% in 1960 to 40.62% in 2010. It is expected to rise to 55.65% by 2025. The tumbling of cultural and religious taboos, and the high cost of traditional burial are attributed to this increase in cremation rate.

> After cremation, depending on your preference, you can scatter the ashes into air, over land, or water. You may scatter the ashes on "private property," "public park," or "at a place that was special to your loved one." You can also bury the cremains or keep them in your home.

> Some common ways of disposal: **Casting:** It means that you simply toss the cremated remains on the wind. **Trenching:** This method involves digging a trench in soil, pouring the ashes in the hole and then covering it with soil. Trenching can also be done on a beach so that the tide washes the remains back to the sea. **Raking:** In this method, the ashes are poured evenly on loose soil and then raked into the ground. **Water scattering** means, dispersing the cremains into a lake, sea or ocean directly or in a *water-soluble urn,* that floats for a few minutes and then slowly sinks or dissolves. **Aerial scattering** requires a professional to cast the ashes from a private plane at a specific location.

36. Procostination

Procrastination can be costly, hence the title of this story.

Mary was admitted to hospice care on the 18th of December. Her two daughters, Nancy and Anna never discussed funeral arrangements for their mother; they decided to contact a funeral home on December 23rd. The funeral director faxed them the papers on Christmas-Eve. Both daughters were caught up in the middle of Christmas preparations, and they did not want to look at funeral papers on Christmas-Eve.

On the day after Christmas, Nancy met with the funeral director and signed up for cremation, with a service and viewing of the body at the funeral home, for a total cost of $4950. She was billed $1000 for renting a casket in which to display the body. She was also charged an additional $295 for the container to place the body inside the rented casket. Nancy signed up for all that without reading the fine print.

When Nancy came home with the documents, Anna was furious. She did not want to spend that kind of money for three hours of *looking at the chemically embalmed body* of her mother. Anna wanted a *direct cremation* which would have cost her just $695. Nancy argued that mom never wanted to be *burned* because she was afraid of fire. This mom was like my patient Jim who did not want to be buried because he was afraid of being *suffocated* in the grave! Nancy's mom and Jim seem to think like my friend Jack who donated all his organs for research, except his eyes. He wanted to *see* where he was going after death!

Since the daughters had never discussed these issues prior to that day, it turned into an emotional battle which left traces of pain, guilt, and regret in its wake. It was too late to ask mom!

Despite plenty of nudging and helping from the hospice professionals, some families refuse to make any funeral arrangements until the patient dies. I have walked into many homes, a few minutes after death occurred, when the house is milling with all kinds of people—family, friends, neighbors, and police officers. The body is in the bedroom. In the midst of noise and emotion, I see a family member on the telephone talking to a funeral director.

Funeral directors ask for basic information, such as date of birth, social security number, discharge papers from the military(if any), information about next of kin, type of relationship, home address, phone number, etc., before they can come to the house to remove the body. When you are grieving and the mind is clogged with emotions, and your memory is faulty, you don't want to answer all those questions. You are likely to make on-the-spot choices and decisions that you come to regret later.

Making advance funeral arrangements can make the final journey a nearly stress-free event. One does not have to wait to get old or sign up for hospice care to do this. Anyone who has the potential to die should think about this topic and should have an exit strategy.

* * *

Ponder and Practice

> *Direct cremation* is a disposition option in which the body is cremated, without a funeral service. Direct cremation is the most economic (affordable) option for disposition.

> The body is cremated after a (72 hour waiting period by Florida State law), and you can use the services of a crematory directly rather than a funeral home, which is much less expensive. The body is cremated in a simple wooden container rather than an expensive casket. There is no *viewing, visitation* or *wake* before the cremation, which eliminates the need for embalming. A *memorial service* may be held at a later date, which eliminates the need for an expensive casket and funeral arrangements

> The total cost of a direct cremation could be under a thousand dollars. A traditional funeral could cost ten thousand dollars. If you have that kind of money to spend, consider donating it to a cause for the "living."

37. Frantic Call

It was a frantic call from a distressed woman with confusing emotions, religious questions, and unreasonable requests. It made me sad and angry, and spoiled my mood, albeit partially, for part of the day.

Her name is Jodi. She is the daughter of Hilda who was a patient on my hospice team. Jodi was calling from New York where she had traveled to visit her dad. She had received news that her mom had just died in Florida.

Jodi had a list of things she needed help with. She confessed that she hadn't made funeral arrangements despite urgings from the social worker and me. We had discussed it with her during our first visit to her mother months ago. That morning, she wanted me to give her the name and phone number of a cremation company with the "lowest fee."

I was angry, but I didn't show it. I was angry not just because she didn't make any prior arrangements, but she wanted to know if cremation was the right to thing to do because she was Catholic. She told me that she had no choice but to do cremation because she had no money for an "expensive burial in the ground." These are issues she should have thought about before her mother died.

The purpose of hospice care is to educate, and prepare families for all aspects of death and dying, cremation, funerals and more. Chaplains and social workers are always able and willing to help. Unfortunately, many caregivers refuse to engage in serious conversations until the last minute, and sometimes never.

Jodi made few other demands which I will describe later. The day and time of the call didn't help either.

It was 6.30 a.m. Saturday. Death-related topics like cremation and funeral were far away from my mind. It was the weekend, when I am supposed to get a break from such so called unpleasant realities of life. Besides, I was getting ready to take my son with autism to the beach for him to participate in the *Surfers for Autism* event. My mind was in beach-mode not hospice-mode.

Jodi was impatient. She was upset that I could not come up with the name of a cremation place and for suggesting that she should ask the person attending her mother's death for recommendation.

She told me that she was not comfortable with cremation because she was a Catholic and it is not allowed by the Church. I told her that the Church now permits cremation for Catholics but she didn't seem convinced.

The Catechism of the Catholic Church devotes a single sentence to cremation: "The Church permits cremation, provided that it does not demonstrate a denial of faith in the resurrection of the body."

In 1963, the Vatican lifted the cremation ban. Since 1997, cremated remains (cremains) have been allowed to be present at funeral Masses, and are given the same respect as remains in a casket.

My attempt to educate Jodi about Church policy on cremation fell on deaf ears because she was too emotional to participate in any rational conversation.

She was also bothered by the fact that her mother died without receiving the *Last Rites*. Months ago, I had suggested giving her mother *Last Rites* but Jodi resisted, believing (wrongly) that *Last Rites* hastened the last days. Jodi asked me if I could go to the assisted living facility that morning, and give her mother the *Last Rites*. I told her that the sacrament is given to a patient prior to death, and giving *Last Rites* to a dead body is inappropriate. She was not ready to hear that answer. "I am too emotional to talk now, I need to go," and she abruptly disconnected the phone.

I am not happy when anyone ends a conversation with me in anger and frustration. The chance of that happening is extremely rare, as I am careful not to say or do anything to upset people. It bothered me however, that the conversation with Jodi ended abruptly and I felt helpless to offer the answers she wanted or the support she needed.

Jodi was having a rough time. She is an only child who had to take on the role of caregiver for her elderly parents. Her parents used to live in the same house in New York. In early 2015, it became impossible for them to live together, because her mother had moods and behaviors that made it hard for her father to deal with. Her father was still active, playing golf, and going out with his buddies. He had no patience for his wife who had mood swings, and early symptoms of dementia. So, Jodi decided to move her mother to an assisted living facility in Florida near where she lived and worked.

Jodi traveled between Florida and New York to attend to the needs of both of her parents as best as she could. She was so upset that her mother died when she was away. "I brought her to live near me and she dies when I am not there." I comforted her by saying that she did the best she could under the circumstances, and that she should not beat herself up for not being able to be present when her mom passed.

I have great empathy for the Jodis of the world who have the impossible task of taking care of elderly parents. It is a difficult task in the best of circumstances. But when parents are unreasonable in their demands, and living in separate locations, the caregiver's stress level spikes. That is all the more reason to make pre-arrangements for the affairs of the elderly before everything reaches crisis point.

Jodi's discomfort about cremation could have been discussed and processed in detail, had she taken up my offer to meet with her after my first visit to her mother. I also could have helped her clarify her misconceptions about the Sacrament of the Sick (Last Rites) and her mother could have been anointed under much different circumstances.

If you are a caregiver for the elderly, heed this advice: *Prepare...prepare...prepare in advance to avoid unnecessary heartache and avoidable adversity.*

* * *

Ponder and Practice

> "Failing to plan is planning to fail."

> I know a young couple who bought two burial plots using part of the money they received as wedding gifts in 1955. They were patients on my hospice team in 2011. Talk about extreme planning!

> Are you a planner or a freelancer? Think of a time in your life when lack of planning cost you money and caused emotional pain. What lessons did you learn from that if any?

38. Death Row

I think I just placed my mother on death row. As he blurted
out those words, Mike began to cry. Hours earlier, he had signed up
his mother for hospice care. The fact that it was an agonizing
decision for Mike was all too apparent. What is also apparent in that
statement is total ignorance about the nature and scope of hospice
care. The misunderstandings, misconceptions, and myths about
hospice care are too many to narrate in this story.

Despite its enormous advantages, hospice is still a mystery to
most Americans. It is primarily because of our society's resistance to
talk about matters related to death. But the irony is that hospice care
is more about life and less about death—quality of life at the end of
life.

For months, Mike was advised by his mother's doctor to
explore hospice care for her. He resisted for a long time. Finally,
when he signed her up, he was confused and conflicted.

It was time for a conversation. First of all, I had to dispel the
notion that hospice is a place or a building. I told him that hospice is
not about giving up on life but about enhancing life. It doesn't mean
stopping all medical care. It is about giving up aggressive medical
care such as chemotherapy in case of cancer, dialysis in case of
kidney disease, or feeding tube to keep a patient artificially alive.
Pain management—one of the prime goals of hospice—is to help a
patient be comfortable rather than suffer or be sedated.

I also told him that hospice care can enrich the last stage of
his mother's life. Instead of admitting her to a hospital, and being
hooked up to machines that do very little to halt the dying process,

his mother could be cared for in the comfort of her home, allowing nature to take its course. I informed Mike that hospice was less about the medical diagnosis but more about the spiritual aspect of life at this very important stage in his mother's life.

Mike was surprised to hear that hospice care was fully covered by *Medicare*. He was worried about the financial cost of the service. When I told him that his mother would also receive a hospital bed, a wheelchair, a commode, and supplies such as diapers and wipes, he thought I was kidding.

I also explained to him that the service is for the entire family to help them cope with the unknown and unfamiliar aspects of end of life issues. For example, having a nurse at the bedside of your loved one to explain and interpret the signs of imminent death can be of great benefit for the family. In short, hospice helps people with terminal diagnosis to live fully rather than die early.

At the end of our conversation, Mike seemed convinced that he had made the right decision for his mother who was 95 years old. In the past three months, she had grown frail and weak. She had lost weight and was mostly confined to her bed. She had no interest in eating and had little energy for engaging in any serious conversations. She was ready *to go*, but Mike was not prepared to let her go.

After being under the care of our hospice team for two months, Mike's mother died peacefully. During that period, she got weekly visits from our team nurse, monthly visits from our team social worker and myself. She also received personal care from a home-health-aide, three times a week. Mike received phone calls from the nurse, social worker and me updating him of his mother's condition and offering him emotional support.

During the last three days of her life when death was deemed imminent, his mother also received round-the-clock crisis care (also known as continuous care) from LPNs, providing comfort care. It was comforting for Mike too because he could relax a bit knowing that his mother was in caring, compassionate, capable, professional hands.

I officiated at funeral services for his mother. The service was personal and tailor-made because I had the opportunity to develop a relationship with the patient and the family. Mike was extremely happy about the care his mother received. "I don't know what I would have done without you guys," he wondered.

In the service comment of the post-hospice survey, Mike wrote in big letters: "Hospice care is the best-kept-secret of our time."

* * *

Ponder and Practice

> What are your personal feelings about hospice? Did this story help clarify some of your questions? Learn more about hospice by visiting **www.*Vitas.com*** or ***www.hospice.org***

> If you were to receive a terminal diagnosis from your doctor, would you choose hospice care for yourself?

> "Death has been with you every moment of your life; you have survived thousands of deaths every day as your old thoughts, your old cells, your old emotions, and even your old identity passed away. Everyone is living in the after-life right now."

~ Deepak Chopra

39. Existing *versus* Living

When is a good time to let go?

I know of a patient who, at the age of 63, suffered a traumatic brain injury, and has been in a coma for seven years. The machines do the breathing for her and she gets tubal feeding. She also gets 24 hour care from private aides. Her family members refuse to remove the feeding tube because they think doing so is akin to *starving* her. They are hesitant to unplug the machines, which they feel is akin to *killing* her.

The field of bioethics is complex and complicated. I do not want to enter the quagmire of varying views and opinions on this issue. But after having worked in hospice, especially with the elderly population, I believe that the terminally ill and the elderly should be helped to die with peace and dignity, rather than enabling them prolong their *existence* in pain, loneliness, agony, and despair. The use of the word *existence* was intentional, because they are merely *existing*, not *living,* which implies engagement with the environment.

Let us take the case of Mary, 90, who is admitted to hospice with a diagnosis of congestive heart failure. She is oriented to her name only. In hospice, we talk about triple orientation: awareness of one's identity, location, and time. Mary does not know where she is or what day, date, month, or year it is. She is tired, confused, and irritable most of the time. She has been in the hospice program for 22 months. During my first visit, when she was alert, she told me that she was tired of living and wanted to die. As the disease progressed, she was unable to even articulate that feeling due to lack of energy and inability to speak.

Mary lives in an Alzheimer's unit with 25 other residents, all in wheelchairs. The unit is understaffed with home health aides who are pulled in all directions by the constant demands of residents who need to be washed, changed, fed, and supervised.

For most of the day, Mary sits in front of a television with colorful images and sound, which fail to evoke any reaction of delight or disgust for her, because her eyes are closed. Even if they were open, I don't think she can process what is going on in front of her. Mary does not have short-term memory. She may have long-term memory, but she cannot draw from it to articulate anything. It is my 19th visit to Mary, but for her, it is the first, because she cannot recall that she had met me before.

In computer terms, Mary has neither *memory* nor *save* functions in her brain.

Mary always seemed sad or bitter. If I remember anything close to a smile on her face, it was a painful smile. Her demeanor conveyed the image of a *dead woman walking,* sitting down.

Mary was taking 19 different medications for a variety of conditions. I have always wondered about the wisdom of giving all those pills to a 90 year old hospice patient when 9.5 million people die in the world each year due to infectious diseases, because they can't afford the medicine. Sitting in front of someone like Mary is a clear case of blessed unrest in my heart. Yes, I am blessed to be alive; yes, I am blessed to be living in a country with enough food, comfortable shelter, and plenty of clothes. My basic needs are met above and beyond my expectations. I feel bad about the millions of people in the world whose basic needs are not met. I am heart-broken about my next door neighbor in India who committed suicide by jumping in front of a train, because he could not afford the medicine to treat his skin disease.

Mary does not have any extended family except for her daughter Linda, who lives out of state. She only visits once a year, more out of obligation than out of affection. She has her own life and issues to deal with. It is sad that the elderly, who are ignored and abandoned by family, are condemned to a life of loneliness in *assisted living facilities* where, ironically, nothing is facile.

Mary's daughter was surprised that her 90 year old mother was being given 19 different pills. She was flabbergasted when she saw the bill for two weeks of critical care—a whopping twenty four thousand dollars! She thought hospice was *milking* Medicare.

When politicians talk about the *sanctity of life,* and urge others to take extraordinary measures to keep patients alive, their prime concern is often love of money rather than love of life. Many people are not aware of the impact of perverse economic incentives within medicine. The health care industry lobby, made up of hospitals, doctors, pharmaceutical companies, and device and product manufacturers, is very powerful politically.

According to Katy Butler, author of *Knocking on Heaven's Door: A Path to a Better Way of Death*, "between 1998 and 2011, pharmaceutical companies and makers of health products spent $2.3 billion on lobbying, making them the single biggest influencer of members of Congress, who in turn pressure Medicare and other federal agencies to create regulations to conform to lobbyists' interests, sometimes to the detriment of patients."

As she poignantly points out, *most of us say we don't want to die plugged into machines, but a fifth of American deaths now take place in intensive care, where ten days of futile flailing can cost as much as $323,000.*

In her book, Ms. Butler explores how our *terror of death* collides with the technological imperatives of modern medicine. Her provocative thesis is that *advanced medicine, in its single-minded pursuit of maximum longevity, often creates more suffering than it prevents.*

I am a witness to that reality every day!

* * *

Ponder and Practice

> How long would you like to live if you were dependent on a feeding tube and ventilator? How long would you keep a loved one in that condition?

> What are your thoughts about giving 19 pills to a 90 year old patient for conditions like high blood pressure, depression, and to increase her appetite?

> Read Katy Butler's book: *Knocking on Heaven's Door: A Path to a Better Way of Death.*

40. Kevorkian Syndrome

Mary's daughter Linda asked me if I would support her decision to discontinue all medications except the ones needed for comfort, because she knew that withholding meds was a passive way of hastening her mother's death. She wanted to make sure that the chaplain would support her. I said *yes,* which brings me to the theological and spiritual issues of the situation.

Mary has come to the last chapter of her life. Does that chapter have to be boring, gloomy, and sad? At this point, she is not living but merely existing. Her existence mainly consists of three half-eaten pureed meals shoved into her mouth by a frenzied aide, and three diaper changes a day. She is barely present to the life unfolding around her and even within her. She is unconscious of the past, unexcited about the future, and is spending endless days sitting in a wheelchair, staring at a bare wall, while being irritated by the idiosyncrasies of fellow residents. Mary doesn't seem to appreciate this kind of *living,* and her daughter, won't mind her mother's existence coming to its conclusion.

Linda must have felt like Anton Chekhov, a famous writer and physician who died of tuberculosis in 1904. He wrote: *Whenever there is someone in a family who has long been ill, and hopelessly ill, there comes painful moments when all, timidly, secretly, at the bottom of their hearts, long for his death.*

Mary's daughter is running out of money. She won't be able to keep her mom at her current placement for more than six months. This is a problem faced by many caregivers of the elderly nationwide. According to the CBO, ten thousand people are turning 65 every day in this country and that will continue for the next fifteen years until the last baby boomer reaches that age. Life expectancy has increased by 15 years beyond what was projected by the government when Social Security was established in 1935. It is estimated that a quarter of Medicare's annual outlays covers medical care in the last year of life. As a nation, will we be able to sustain the level of care we provide for the elderly to prolong their existence?

This is not just an American problem. People are living longer in all parts of the world. That is why Tara Aso, Japanese finance minister, bemoaning the financial burden that caring for the elderly in their final years places on the country's budget, said this: "The problem won't be solved unless you let them hurry up and die."

It is in this larger context of the patient situation, caregiver dilemma, and economic data that I experience symptoms of *Kevorkian Syndrome*. Dr. Kevorkian was a Michigan doctor who advocated and implemented assisted suicide. Are we doing a favor for Mary by keeping her body alive while her ability and will to live has vanished? Is it possible that when she says *I want to go home...take me home*, she is asking us to take her to her eternal home? When other patients ask me if I had a pill for them or find a gun for them, aren't they expressing a desire to end the life they don't savor anymore?

In most cases, the extremely elderly and the grievously injured are kept alive by elaborate, costly, and increasingly heroic medical procedures. Despite knowing that there is no quality of life to such medically induced existence, caregivers are reluctant to let go of their loved ones. Author Andy Crouch describes such life as living in the "uncanny valley of the shadow of death." According to Crouch, *life in this uncanny valley's shadow is neither death nor life. It calls forth mourning but also forbids it. It offers the slimmest of hopes, but in many, if not most cases, it slowly squeezes hope out of life one mechanically induced breath at a time.*

I am not a fan of Jack Kevorkian's flamboyant techniques for assisted suicide. I cannot say, however, I am totally against the idea of letting people *go home* in cases where the patient has lost the will to live and only a plethora of medications, artificial feeding, and machine hook-ups will prolong life.

It is not disregard for the elderly to acknowledge the fact that 90 year old bodies don't bounce back like the body of a 19 year old. It is not disrespect for life to admit that death is a necessary and inevitable part of life, no matter how many pills are pushed and how much technology is implemented. I am not challenging the authority of God as the creator of life, but claiming our responsibility as co-creators with God.

A recent essay by Dr. Zeke Emmanuel titled, *Why I Hope to Die at 75,* raises some very interesting points about our reluctance to face our mortality. "Doubtless, death is a loss…but here is a simple truth that many of us seem to resist: living too long is also a loss."

Debbie, the daughter of one of my patients, who takes care of her 98 year old father attests to this. She says that she "lost" her father years ago to Alzheimer's. Debbie calls her dad "an eating, sleeping, pooping machine."

* * *

Ponder and Practice

> When someone insisted that there could be only one *absolutely* right answer to any given moral question, the Master said:

"When people sleep in a damp place they get lumbago. But that's not true of fish."

"Living on a tree can be perilous and trying on the nerves. But that's not true of monkeys."

"So of these three, fish and monkeys and humans, whose habitat is *absolutely* the right one?" "Human beings eat flesh, buffaloes grass, and tress feed on the earth. Of these three, whose taste is the right one—*absolutely*?" ~ Anthony De Mello

41. Death with Dignity

The case of Brittany Maynard, a 29 year old newly-wed who was diagnosed with brain tumor— *glioblastoma multiform*—is an inspiring and controversial story. She moved from California to Oregon where *Death with Dignity* laws exist, to die with dignity rather than prolong her agony while experiencing the ravages of her disease. In a video message to her friends, she said: *When my suffering becomes too great, I can say to all those I love: I love you, come be by my side, and come say goodbye as I pass into whatever is next. I will die upstairs in my bedroom with my husband, mother, stepfather, and best friend by my side and pass peacefully. I can't imagine trying to rob anyone else of that choice.*

A Vatican's top bioethics official condemned Brittany Maynard's euthanasia as "reprehensible." I think that was a cruel assessment and a heartless comment from a man who lives in an ivory tower thousands of miles away from the agonizing situation of this young woman and her family. Brittany's mother Debbie Ziegler was so upset about that remark that she wrote an open letter to all those who condemned her daughter's agonizing decision:

I am Brittany Maynard's mother. I am writing in response to a variety of comments made in the press and online by individuals and institutions that have tried to impose their personal belief system on what Brittany and our family feel is a human rights issue.

*The imposition of "belief" on a human rights issue is wrong. To censure a personal choice as **reprehensible** because it does not comply with someone else's belief is immoral. My twenty-nine-year-old daughter's choice to die gently rather than suffer physical and mental degradation and intense pain does not deserve to be labeled as **reprehensible** by strangers a continent away who do not know her or the particulars of her situation.*

Reprehensible is a harsh word meaning "very bad; deserving very strong criticism." Reprehensible is a word I've used as a teacher to describe the actions of Hitler, other political tyrants and the exploitation of children by pedophiles. As Brittany Maynard's mother, I find it difficult to believe that anyone who knew her would ever select this word to describe her actions. Brittany was a giver. She was a volunteer. She was a teacher. She was an advocate. She worked at making the world a better place in which to live.

This word was used publicly at a time when my family was tender and freshly wounded: Grieving. Such strong public criticism from people we do not know, and have never met—is more than a slap in the face. It is like kicking us as we struggle to draw a breath.

People and institutions that feel they have the right to judge Brittany's choices may wound me and cause me unspeakable pain, but they do not deter me from supporting my daughter's choice. There is currently a great deal of confusion and arrogance standing in the way of Americans going gently into the good night. I urge Americans to think for themselves. Make your wishes clear while you are competent. Make sure that you have all the options spelled out for you, if you are diagnosed with an incurable, debilitating, painful disease. Do your own research. Ask your family to research and face the harsh reality with you. Ask your doctor to be brutally honest with you. Then make your personal choice about how you will proceed. It is YOUR choice.

The "culture of cure" has led to a fairy tale belief that doctors can always fix our problems. We have lost sight of reality. All life ends. Death is not necessarily the enemy in all cases. Sometimes a gentle passing is a gift. Misguided doctors caught up in an aspirational belief that they must extend life, whatever the cost, cause individuals and families unnecessary suffering. Brittany stood up to bullies. She never thought anyone else had the right to tell her how long she should suffer. The right to die for the terminally ill is a human rights issue. Plain and simple.

The Vatican bioethics official added that "suicide is a bad thing because it is saying no to life and to everything it means with respect to our mission in the world and towards those around us," describing assisted suicide as "an absurdity."

Let us clarify a few things: First of all, Brittany didn't commit suicide. Suicide is a desperate act, committed usually by mentally ill people who see life as hopeless and pointless. Brittany Maynard was anything but. "There is not a single cell in my body that is suicidal," she said. This woman wanted to live so badly. She was just 29 and newly married. She wanted children with her husband. Death was far from her mind. But when confronted with the inevitable and savage suffering that would surely ravage her body and mind, she chose to die with dignity, which I believe is a courageous decision.

The Pope and the Vatican official speak from the false notion that suffering is good in itself, and they point to the suffering of Jesus on the cross as a point of reference for all sufferings. Jesus did not suffer on the cross for the sake of suffering. Suffering was inflicted upon him by the religious and political authorities of his day. Jesus turned that suffering into a redemptive act. So, suffering undertaken for a higher cause, and as a result of a higher calling is both redemptive and sublime. But to suffer, just for the sake of it, is merely masochistic.

Another argument against euthanasia is that God is the creator of life. That is true—partially. The full truth is that we and God are co-creators of life. Without human intention and participation, no new life will be born, regardless of how hard God tries. This is not an arrogant stance of an unbeliever or an atheist but the humble opinion of a committed disciple who takes his identity as an image of God seriously, and his calling as God's co-creator, responsibly.

I have had many conversations with my wife on the topic of end-of- life care. She knows that I don't want to live an extra day on this planet if I have to consume countless pills or be hooked up to machines for my survival. I am a firm believer in the Buddhist wisdom of *detachment* which makes it easy for me not to cling to anything in life, including life itself.

I am neither impervious to the *sanctity of life* argument nor the danger of the *slippery slope* approach. Therefore I will always advocate for the cause of *life* but the pragmatist in me struggles to find convincing reasons to fight for mere *existence.*

* * *

Ponder and Practice

> What do you think of Brittany's choice? In a similar situation, would you choose that?

> Think of the ways your life will change if you were to change your identity and role from being a mere *creature of* God, to *Co-creator with* God.

> What do you think of Brittany's mother's letter to the Vatican? How do you feel about politicians and religious leaders who don't know your life situation, regulating and pontificating about your life?

42. D.N.R. Dilemma

During my on-call shift one Sunday afternoon, I was dispatched to "attend the death" of one our patients. "Attending death" in our hospice program involves arriving at the house, pronouncing the patient, comforting the family, disposing of controlled substances, calling the funeral home, staying with the family until the body is removed, providing continued support to family if needed, and making a report to the hospice office.

When I arrived at Molly's house, a frantic man came running to the door, panting and crying because he "could not save his mother." When Molly experienced difficulty breathing, her son Scott panicked and called the hospice office. He was placed on hold to find a nurse, but waiting even thirty seconds watching his mother gasping for breath was like an eternity. So Scott hung up with the hospice office and dialed 911.

The dispatcher told him to give CPR to his mother. He was advised to move his mother from the bed to the floor and compress her chest. At first Scott could only do it with one hand as he had to hold the phone in the other, to listen to the dispatcher's instructions. Scott had never done CPR before nor had any training. When the dispatcher told him to increase the pressure, Scott put his phone down and pressed the chest of his mother very hard with both hands. He worried he broke her ribs.

When I arrived, I saw the lifeless body of his mother Molly on the floor, wearing a diaper and a T-shirt. I checked her pulse, pronounced her dead, and covered her body with a clean sheet. I offered to say a prayer but Scott declined by saying: "What is the use now, she is dead."

Molly was 92 years old. She was a cancer survivor, with a diagnosis of heart disease and diabetes. She was placed on hospice care two weeks prior to her death. Her son, Scoot who is 66, refused to sign the DNR because he thought he was "giving up on his mother too soon." This is a common sentiment among some care-givers, because DNR is often viewed as a "deadly" document with negative implications.

Do Not Resuscitate is a negative directive with a positive intent, and many people think that it is akin to watching someone die without offering a helping hand. In fact, it is a "compassionate document." There have been discussions in medical circles to change its negative connotation by renaming it A.N.D—Allow Natural Death. The emotions surrounding this document often lead to unnecessary harm to patients, and untold stress for caregivers.

Scott felt terrible that he had to press so hard on his mother's chest to no avail. He felt bad about putting her through the indignity of dragging her out of her bed and placing her on a bare floor. At the end, he felt helpless and hopeless.

I am empathetic towards Scott and caregivers like him. No one should have to go through what Scott had to experience. Educating the public about the nature of hospice care in general, and the importance of documents like the DNR in particular, are sorely needed to avoid such traumatic experiences in critical times.

I believe that it is a terrible idea to administer CPR to a patient with Molly's age and health profile. Since comfort care is the purpose of hospice, why bring discomfort to the patient by pressing her chest so hard, often at the risk of breaking the ribs? In the case of elderly and fragile patients, it is extremely risky.

It is also important to realize that by signing a DNR, caregivers are actually doing a huge favor to their loved ones by allowing nature to take its course rather than trying to control the outcome, often to no avail.

* * *

Ponder and Practice

> COPD (Chronic Obstructive Pulmonary Disease) is the third leading cause of death in the United States. More than 11 million people have been diagnosed with COPD, but an estimated 24 million may have the disease without even knowing it.

> Some caregivers think of DNR as a death warrant. Consider it as the most humane document, especially in the case of hospice patients.

> Human lungs breathe in and out about 2100 to 2400 gallons of air every day. The total length of the airways running through the two lungs is 1500 miles...and the lungs have about 300 million alveolies (air sacs). Bend your mental knees before the Maker of this miraculous machine and say a prayer of gratitude.

43. Strangers Are Family

It was 4 p.m. Sunday and my on-call shift had just started. I was sent to a nursing home to attend a death. "Attending death" in our hospice vernacular, means offering comfort to the family, making arrangements to transfer the body to the funeral home, and informing related parties. The patient's name was Sadie and I was told that her daughter Stacy was her caregiver. With that information and the address of the nursing home in hand, I began to drive.

When I walked in, I saw a lady talking on the phone who was the patient's daughter. I introduced myself as the chaplain from *Vitas Hospice*. She looked suspiciously at me wondering (I guess) why a chaplain was coming to attend the death of a Jewish patient. I gave her a hug and expressed my condolences. She took me into the room where her mother's body was. Her two sons were at the bedside. After a few brief words of condolences, I asked them if they would like me to say a prayer. They said "yes" and we held hands, and I offered a prayer for bliss for Sadie and peace for the family.

As soon as the prayer ended, son Gary asked me: "Is there any way you could do the funeral for our mom?"

I was shocked and surprised. Normally, Jewish families seek out a Rabbi to officiate funerals even if the family is only culturally Jewish.

Stacy, Gary, and Richard had only known me five minutes, and I had never met them before. Yet, I felt totally at home with them, and they seemed to feel the same. I told them a little about my philosophy that all humans are the same at the core, and there are more things that unite us than divide us. Quoting Mitch Albom, I also told them that *strangers are family you haven't met, yet.* We talked for a while about their mom and how mom's prolonged illness had brought the siblings together.

On Tuesday morning, we gathered for Sadie's funeral—just the four of us. It was an intimate ceremony, conducted in the Jewish tradition. They were pleasantly surprised that a Christian chaplain knew about the Jewish tradition, and even attempted to say the *Kaddish prayer* in Hebrew. Gary told me that I could easily pass for a Rabbi. I appreciated the compliment.

At the end of the service, we hugged each other before Stacy, Gary, and Richard parted for Connecticut, Philadelphia, and New York. They requested that I mark my calendar for a day in May 2016 for the *Unveiling* when the grandchildren and other extended family will travel to Florida.

Before parting, I told them that I felt like being part of their family. "The feeling is mutual," said Gary. I told Stacy that I had three sisters in India and I miss them. She said she would be happy to be a stand-in-sister for me in the USA.

While walking towards my car I thought about the mysterious ways of God that connected me to the lives of three more spiritual siblings.

Two weeks after the funeral, I received a beautiful card from Stacy:

Dearest Paul:

Amid all the many things going on right now, I wanted to make this time to thank you so very much for your kindness, warmth and support that you extended to me and my family following my mom's death. You sincerely and beautifully helped with some closure that my brothers and I desperately needed. I thank you again for everything and will think of you always with much fondness.

Best wishes always.

With love and gratefulness.

Stacy Soto.

P.S. I have two great brothers but I wish I was your sister too!

* * *

Ponder and Practice

> According to the Human Genome Project Study (2003), all humans are 99.9 percent identical. It means that only 0.1 percent of our genes account for the differences between individuals! Let that awareness guide your relationship with humanity.

> Develop the awareness that *separation* between humans is an *illusion*, and you will immediately feel ease in your interactions with people, and establish connections easily.

> Acknowledge your "Divine paternity" and *see* spiritual siblings all around! "If we have no peace, it is because we have forgotten that we belong to each other." ~ Mother Teresa

44. Mondays with Morris

On March 14, 2016, Morris turned 100 years old—a Jewish man born and raised in Brooklyn, New York. Our biographies were different, and our theologies didn't match, but our hearts were in unison with all that really matters in life—love and compassion for humanity. Instantly, I fell in love with Morris who exuded joy, emanated peace and enjoyed people. His sense of humor and generous spirit are extremely rare among patients of his age and diagnosis. He was happy and content. Although his body was weak, his mind was sharp, and he could engage in meaningful conversations.

During the last two years in hospice care, I have visited Morris once a month, mostly on Mondays. He provided me with the mental boost I needed for the week. I call this story *Mondays with Morris* because of its similarities to elements of Mitch Albom's book, *Tuesdays with Morrie—an old man, a young man and life's greatest lesson.* Even on his deathbed, Morrie the *mensch* taught Mitch how to live robustly and fully. Morris has done the same for me during the last two years of my interactions with him.

One day, during a life-review session, I asked Morris, "What is the secret of a happy life?" and he replied: "Serve people."

Morris served in the US Air force for 24 years. For 11 years, he was a draw-bridge operator in Florida. For 8 hours a day, five days a week, he had to manage the bridge on the intra-coastal waterway, to let boats pass underneath it. He did that job joyfully because he was serving people. When I asked him if he felt jealous of the rich people in those boats who were having fun and he had to do his apparently monotonous job, he said: "I had my fun when I was young, I don't begrudge them having fun."

For 17 years, he volunteered at the Veteran's Hospital in Miami. One of his duties was to organize the Bingo games. "Seeing happiness on the face of others is my happiness," he said.

Me: "If you could travel to one more place or do one more thing, what would that be?"

Morris: "I would like to go to Haiti and help the people. They are poor people living there. They are nice people. The aide who takes care of me is from Haiti. I love her."

Other patients have replied to similar questions with answers such as: "I want to take one more cruise;" or "I want to go for one more vacation to Europe."

Me: "How do you find joy in a boring place like this assisted living facility?"

Morris: "I look forward to everyday as a blessing. At my age, any day could be my last day, so I take advantage of every minute I have left."

Me: "You are totally dependent on others for your survival; how can that be a *blessing*?"

Morris: "I am still breathing and I am not hungry; that is a blessing."

I sat in front this old man examining my own feelings and attitude towards life. At age 65, I have an over-flow of blessings in all areas of my life, and yet I am not grateful enough. I hope I would think and feel and behave like Morris when I reach his age. Morris humbles me, challenges me, inspires me, and confirms my conviction that serving others is the best route to true happiness. He is an amazing example and ultimate witness to aging gracefully.

At the end of the visit, I take his hand in mine, and say a prayer thanking God for sending this *mensch* into my life. And I am not leaving his presence without getting his blessing. So I bent down, and Morris places his hand on my head, and does a silent blessing.

As I raise my head, my eyes are brimming with tears of gratitude and joy, and I see a set of twinkling eyes "speaking" the universal language of pure love.

As I leave his room, Morris says: "May you live to see 100 years like me."

* * *

Ponder and Practice

> *An unexamined life is not worth living,* said Socrates. Articulate in ten words or less your basic philosophy of life.

> If you could visit one more place before you die, where would that be, and why?

> "Not all of us can do great things, but all of us can do small things with great love." ~Mother Teresa

45. Can I Have Some Chips?

At age 30, Keisha was diagnosed with AIDS, which she contracted from unprotected sex with a partner who was callous and irresponsible. She sat on her bed staring at the wall, visibly depressed. She had spent two years fighting her illness, denying it, being angry with herself, and bargaining with God for a miraculous cure. When her doctor recommended hospice, Keisha knew it was the beginning of the end. The prospect of dying at the young age of thirty two was devastating.

During my visit, Keisha was nervous because she was afraid that I would judge her for having AIDS, a disease often associated with sexual promiscuity. Keisha's mother invited me to sit on the bed as there was no chair in their one bedroom apartment. Keisha's mother spoke about their poverty, deprivation and dependence, and the fears about the impending death of her only daughter. My heart was filled with sadness and tender love for this dying young woman. I felt a connection with her which is hard to explain, a feeling of empathy and love, as if she were my own little sister.

Keisha and her mother came to the United States from Peru nine years ago. They lived as illegal immigrants, and never obtained *Green Cards*. Keisha's mother worked menial jobs and depended on the good will of family and friends for survival. Keisha did not complete school, hung out with the wrong crowd, and ended up ill and destitute. This family was three months behind on their rent and did not have a dollar in their purse on the day of my visit.

Keisha's mother showed me an album with pictures of happier times. Keisha used to weigh about 130 pounds, but she was a frail woman now, weighing only 72 pounds.

While I was perusing through the album, Keisha began to cry. "I am a bad person and God is going to punish me," she said. She seemed visibly afraid of the punishment of God awaiting her. I told her that the God I know is a loving father who never punishes anyone. I told her the story of the prodigal son in Chapter 15 of the Gospel of Luke, a story of compassion, forgiveness, and unconditional love.

At the end of the visit, we held hands and I prayed that the Lord hold Keisha in the palm of His hand, embrace her in love, touch and heal her, comfort her, and fill her heart with peace—a peace which the world cannot give or take away. I hugged her and whispered in her ear: "Jesus loves you," the affirmation of a promise of love for every person, regardless of his or her status in life. She seemed relieved and relaxed, at least for a moment.

Before leaving, I asked Keisha if there was anything else I could help with, and she said: "I like to eat a bagel and some ice cream." But they had no money. Buying a bagel and ice cream for a dying woman was the least I could do. I gave them what I had in my wallet, and told her mother to buy bagel and ice cream for her daughter.

"Is there anything else you would like to eat"? I asked: "I like chips," she said. Another very simple request. I promised her that she would have some chips by the next day.

I visited Keisha again, this time with a bag of 24 varieties of chips from *Sam's Club*. Her face lit up and she held on to that bag until I left. Being so weak, Keisha could hardly say, "Thank you sir."

I wiped my tears—tears of gratitude for blessing me by bringing Keisha into my life; tears of sadness that she wouldn't be around for long.

I was humbled and mystified that something as simple as potato chips could be a source of blessing in my life.

* * *

Ponder and Practice

> A business executive asked what the Master thought was the secret of successful living.

Said the Master, "Make one person happy each day."

As an afterthought he added, "Even if that person is yourself."

A minute passed and he said, "Especially if that person is yourself."

~Anthony De Mello

> At a fast food drive-through window, pay for the customer behind you.

> Make sure you smile each time you see another human being, regardless of the place and circumstances. Your smile will light up the world around you!

46. My Terrible Sins

Rose was a patient on my team for two years. In the beginning, she was able to communicate in short sentences and respond to simple questions. She used to sit in her wheelchair for hours. As weeks and months went by, she was unable to hold her head up. I would see her hunched over with her head resting on the table in front of her.

When I visit, she would raise her head, take my hand in hers and just hold it for a long time, and sometimes just kiss it. She liked the warmth of human contact in a place of monotonous routines, utter loneliness, and ultimate abandonment—the locked unit of Alzheimer patients.

Towards the end, it became impossible for Rose to sit up, and she was bedridden. During my visit prior to her death, Rose was resting comfortably but her eyes were open and she was alert.

"What are you thinking about, Rose? I asked.

"My sins" she replied.

"Would you like to talk?"

"They are terrible sins. I don't know if God would forgive me."

There was fear, sadness, and helplessness in Rose's eyes. I had no curiosity about her sins. I wanted to offer comfort to her in the best way I could. So, I spoke these words:

Rose I want you to know that God loves you; God has loved you all along, from the day you were born, to this moment…90 long years of unconditional love for you. There was not a moment in your life that God was away from you. The "terrible sins" you are thinking about are no a match for the tremendous mercy of God that is being poured out on you this moment. God doesn't think about your past, imperfect as it might have been. He sees your heart and is blessing you at this time. Be at peace.

I traced the sign of the cross on her forehead, held her hand, and said a prayer for peace and healing.

Rose opened her eyes, her face lit up with a beautiful smile; she pressed and kissed my hand and said: "Thank you."

For many patients, sins, regrets, and punishment are death bed issues. Heaven and hell are considered as post-death destinations. If you are a Catholic, add purgatory to the list as a possible place you could end up after death for a period of time.

But does anybody *"go* to any of those *places?"* What *goes?* To *where?* Obviously the body is going underground or to the oven. The soul does not need a place or location. Are these actual *locations* behind pearly gates or under the crust of the earth? I'm not sure.

Is it possible that the sufferings that we face during this life are punishment enough for our sins? I believe in consequences of our actions, not in punishments.

Eternal punishment for *temporal* deeds makes no sense.

What lies beyond death is pure mystery.

* * *

Ponder and Practice

> Do you believe in Divine punishment and judgment?

> Imagine you entering heaven and noticing that Hitler is in heaven too. How would that make you feel?

> Is there anyone in your life who you need to forgive? Or do you need someone to forgive you? Consider offering and/or receiving forgiveness.

47. I Got the Blues

It was an ordinary Monday morning, going to the office, logging on to the computer, and checking the weekend's activity—admissions and discharges of my patients. I saw a name on my screen of someone I knew very well, and with whom I had become friends over the last five years on the music scene in South Florida. It was Don.

I sat in stunned silence for a few minutes, because I was looking at the name of a friend who was a local favorite *Blues/Rock* guitarist, who was now my patient.

The last time I saw Don and his girlfriend was at the *Hard Rock* in Hollywood, in December of 2014. Don talked to me about his fight with colon cancer earlier in the year. He had lost some weight, but overall seemed fine to me. I would see Don perform a week later, for what would be my last time to see him at a local gig.

My stunned silence and ashen face made the chaplain in the adjacent cubicle ask me: "You okay, bro?" I said I was shocked to see my friend as a hospice patient. He was willing to take the patient from me as he thought it must be too personal for me to handle. But I needed to do this. The hour prior to leaving the office for that visit, I was anxious, reflecting on what this meant and what I would say to him upon arrival.

Although I had been a hospice chaplain for five years, I was still adjusting to the routine of dealing with death on a regular basis. I had never really processed the feelings and kept those thoughts bottled up inside. At times I was sad, but I had to tough it out because that's what a good chaplain did, or so I thought.

I remembered reading about Don winning a local Blues competition. I loved live music, especially the Blues. His music was what I needed to hear at the end of a week filled with sadness, some existential anxiety, and my own wondering about the nature of life and death. Listening to his music with some good food and drink on the weekend brought delight to my soul. That was the beginning of a nice friendship, as best one can be without becoming a groupie.

So on the morning of July 13, I headed out towards downtown Fort Lauderdale to join the nurse to visit Don. As we approached the door I felt a heavy heart.

We were ushered in by a nice middle-aged woman, who was Don's ex-wife. I told her I knew Don and then saw his girlfriend, who seemed shocked to see me. She was so glad that I was there and that I would be Don's spiritual guide. After some niceties, she escorted me into the small bedroom. There lay Don with a bandana around his head, where he used to have long flowing golden blonde hair. Don was a bag of bones; a hollow shell of what he was a few months ago. I could hardly distinguish that this was my old friend who at 57, used to look 45, and now looked like he was 85. I thought to myself, what a dreadful disease is cancer.

The family closed the door behind us, and then began what would be many hours I would spend talking to, being with, and at times, crying with a man who I admired more from afar than up close. I wondered how I was going to do this. I decided to trust that God would guide me through this time with whatever I needed.

Don was dying, right in front of me. His friends had amassed an impromptu acoustic jam session at his residence. It was an amazing four hours in what was a final night of Don's closest friends gathering in his honor; and I felt privileged to be the only outsider invited. I sat next to Don most of the night, as friends came and went. Don knew this was the last time.

During my next visit, I told him about the impact of his music on my psyche and well being. I told him that his music really served my soul (and attitude) on many occasions, and that he had brought great inspiration and joy to me, especially after a long work week. His music uplifted me and helped me get ready to do it all over again.

As days and weeks passed, Don became more lethargic and uncomfortable. His once strong booming voice was now just a whisper, so much so that I had to often put my ear to his mouth to hear him. We shared stories about his favorite gigs and the various musicians he had played with over the years, the fun he had, the loves of his life, and about his only child, a daughter, now a woman, also attending to his bedside.

A couple of days later, the call came at 4:40 a.m. Don had just passed in our hospice unit. I got dressed and flew out the door. I stayed with the family for hours until Don was taken to the funeral home. It was a sad day but one of obvious relief as we watched a once virile, handsome, humorous, and talented man leave this world a shell of what he physically once was.

It is hard to watch people die. It is even harder to watch people you know and love die. It forces us to make sense of an event we all must face, to search a little harder for understanding, purpose, and meaning.

I mourn Don's death. I will never be able to see him play live music again. *YouTube* will give me my only respite from missing the music and the man. Don's passing has created a gap in my life where I used to turn for relaxation, distraction, and some fun on the weekends. His death also makes me reflect a little more on the brevity of life; on just how quickly one's life can end; on the importance of making each day and moment count. To become more than just an observer of life, but a participant. To ask myself if I want to battle the small stuff. To realize that I have only today, the moment I'm in, to enjoy and to find meaning.

Don was just two years older than me. He died at the same age as my two grandfathers did, at age 57. Whatever time we get here, it has to be the best we can make it, despite all the trials and tribulations most of us seem to have in life; it is still a gift, one that should never be taken for granted. I'm happy for Don's spirit now, but I still got the Blues!

(By Chaplain Kevin McGee)

* * *

Ponder and Practice

> What are some of your feelings when you hear in the news or read in the paper that a person of your age has died?

> Have you ever had to deal with a situation similar to the one in this story? How did you deal with it? What helped?

> Imagine a scenario in your mind where you are at the bedside of your best friend who is on hospice care. Do a fantasy meditation to flush out the feelings associated with that situation.

48. Last Rites

Mr. M was admitted to hospice with end stage brain cancer, having recently undergone surgery and was not doing well.

When I visited, his wife told me the following story. He was born in Hungary prior to World War II. His parents were righteous gentiles, Roman Catholics, who hid some Jews during the war so they wouldn't be captured and deported by the Nazis. Mr. M served in the Hungarian Army prior to the communist revolution in 1956. Before the revolution, he deserted the army, was captured and sent to prison. He escaped from prison during the revolution and returned home to say goodbye to his mother.

With little more than the clothing he was wearing, he made his way to Trieste, Italy. There he enlisted in the US Navy having been promised citizenship after serving for 5 years.

In 1961, he immigrated to the United States, and in New Orleans, met the woman who would become his wife. She too was Catholic. Throughout his life, he attended church regularly, but after leaving Hungary, he never took Holy Communion, because he did not have a birth certificate or Baptism documentation to prove to the priest that he was Catholic.

Together they approached five Roman Catholic priests who refused to marry them in the church, because of his lack of documentation. Finally in desperation, they went to a Hungarian Catholic Priest, explained their situation, and that priest was even more adamant than the others in his refusal to marry them. They ended up getting married in a civil ceremony in a local courthouse in New Orleans.

For their 54 years of married life, they attended church every Sunday, but never took communion because, even though Mr. M might never have been asked to produce his baptism papers, he didn't feel right to receive communion.

Hearing their story and their devotion to their faith, which never wavered despite the difficulties they encountered, I asked Mrs. M, as her husband was no longer able to speak and minimally responsive, if she would like to have her husband receive the Sacrament of the Sick and holy communion. She was anxious and asked if I was going to tell the priest their story. I assured her that I would, but the priest I knew would be honored to help this soul. I told her the priest was an ex-military chaplain and a colleague.

My friend and colleague chaplain visited the patient that evening and Mr. M received the sacraments and died during the night. In death, he left this earth as a devout Catholic, receiving what he was entitled to since 1956.

(By Rabbi Lawrence M. Schuval)

* * *

Ponder and Practice

> *Last Rites* also known as *Sacrament of the Sick* is one of the seven sacraments of the Catholic Church usually administered by a priest or deacon. Unlike Baptism, Confirmation, and Holy Orders, this sacrament is repeatable.

> Have you ever been ostracized by your religion or a faith community? What are some of the ways of dealing with such a situation?

> "Religion is more about converting and controlling humans, rather than comforting them." What do you think of that statement?

49. God is with Us

Thursday, 6:20 a.m., an 85 year old female dies of cancer. Only one of her children is with her. The other child is across the county, at a different hospital, where the patient's husband, an 86 year old male, dies of leukemia hours earlier. The bodies are removed and the sheets are changed.

But that's not the way it happened. We celebrated these two people, their lives, their family, their faith, and their love as an integral part of that painful morning of sacred passages.

You matter because you are you, and you matter to the end of your life. We will do all we can not only to help you die peacefully, but also to live until you die. *

It is difficult to imagine that these two people could have died apart from each other. Together they had created and provided a home for two loving children. She had been a nurse in Broward County for over 35 years. He had served in the Air Force, off to war even before he turned 18. She had been raised Methodist, but followed him in his Roman Catholic faith.

Anna and Joseph had been married for over 65 years. She had fought cancer for some time, but recently was losing strength, and had been put on a ventilator to help her breathe. Joseph had been struggling with lymphoid leukemia and was severely declining. They were admitted to different hospitals at different times, miles apart, anticipating death.

"Pray, Chaplain," said the Team Manager, "We have a *Romeo and Juliet* story coming and we have to make it happen." And of course the chaplain prayed. He didn't know that already in another hospital, a Catholic chaplain had anointed Anna and prayed with the family.

The chaplain was present when Anna arrived from the other hospital. The chaplain listened as the daughter told the story of her mother's life, and of the life Anna and Joseph had created together. Providing words of assurance and consolation, the chaplain reflected on the presence of God in such shadows. Later, Anna's son arrived with his father. Joseph was moved into the room with Anna— together now, as they had been for so many years. Together now, with both their children.

Standing between the beds of Anna and Joseph, the chaplain prayed with thanksgiving for the many gifts and acts of love created by this couple and given to the world: "May these acts be blessed and multiplied." The chaplain gave thanks for the family and their courage in a difficult time, and asked God's blessing on them. The chaplain acknowledged with gratitude the work of all those who cared for the family and asked blessings upon them. The hospital room became sacred ground.

The son stepped aside with the chaplain and confessed his faith and his gratitude. "God is with us, he has been so very with us tonight. Everything has come together so well, only God could make this happen." The chaplain affirmed his confession. "I have one more thing to ask, if possible, Chaplain. Could we arrange for a priest to give the *Last Rites* for Dad?"

It was now 11:00 p.m. The chaplain assured the son he would try, but that it was late and unlikely until the next day. When the priest answered at St. Helen's church, the chaplain was astounded. When the priest said, "I'll be over within the hour," the chaplain responded, "God is with us."

Shortly after midnight, Joseph died. A few hours later, at his side, Anna died. The son was still giving thanks to God and repeated, "God is with us." "We are grateful for all that you and *Vitas* did for us." He then expressed deep appreciation that the Catholic chaplain who had started with Anna, was also there to provide a memorial service for both parents, thus bringing the solemn occasion into one story of hope and thanksgiving.

It took God and the commitment of many loving *Vitas* team members to create a remarkable—holy—response to this difficult situation. It began with caring and thoughtful team members in admissions. It required the response of an IPU Team Manager who believes that with love, all things are possible and said, "We'll make it happen." It took physicians and therapists willing to stay late. And it required chaplains: chaplains to pray; chaplains to hear the story and tell the story and incorporate the family's story into God's story; chaplains to provide the words of sacrament and blessing; chaplains to reach out to a community priest; and chaplains to console and affirm God's blessing, and to affirm with the son and all the saints, that indeed "God is with us."

* (Dame Cicely Saunders, nurse, physician and writer, and founder of hospice movement (1918 – 2005).

(Chaplain Steven M. Jurgens-Ling)

* * *

Ponder and Practice

> Does it make a difference if *God is with us,* or *We are with God?*

> Have you ever had an experience of God's palpable presence in your life like the one described in this story?

> What is the difference between *believing in God,* and *experiencing* God?"

143

50. A Beautiful Death

I am a music therapist. I've had several powerful music therapy sessions with actively dying patients throughout my career, and they are all memorable. I remember one particular experience working with a patient whose death was imminent.

The family requested some of the songs that I had provided before. The patient was minimally responsive and receiving oxygen. I played some songs in a relaxing, sedative style to create a soothing atmosphere for the patient and the family. I encouraged some quiet sharing and spoke of how much joy these songs and our sessions had brought to the patient.

Everybody was overwhelmed with emotion but the music began to ease some of that tension. I could see the music starting to bring a sense of comfort to the family and the patient. I saw a slowing of the patient's respiration. As I was softly singing their favorite songs, some of the family members were gently singing with me. Then the daughter of the patient requested a song that her mother had sung to her as a lullaby when she was a young child. This was a song that we had sung together many times in our sessions and I knew how important this song was to both the patient and her daughter.

So I started singing the song, *Summertime,* and I remember singing the first verse … *"Summertime and the livin is easy … the fish are jumping and the cotton is high … your daddy's rich and your mama's good lookin... so hush little baby don't you cry."* and then I began the second verse, *"One of these mornings you're gonna rise up singing, spread your wings and take to the sky."*

When I came to that exact point in the lyrics, the patient reached out, took her daughter's hand and lifted up her head a little.

She opened her eyes and looked at her daughter with a slight smile on her face and then she took her last breath....Needless to say, that experience was very powerful and intense, and it moved me deeply.

It reminded me how hearing is often intact till the very end, and that even when patients are seemingly un-responsive, they are still able to hear, especially music. It was very affirming to know that this patient, who was not responding in any overt way, was actively listening to the song. I wondered if it was a coincidence that she chose that precise moment to open her eyes, and have that last moment with her daughter...The session was an emotionally transcendent experience that stays with me to this day. It was indeed a spiritual moment. It was such a powerful moment that provided a great deal of comfort for the patient's daughter who had the privilege to have her mom die in her arms.

That experience prompted me to write a song about it as a way of processing the experience.

A Beautiful Death

The family was all gathered round
In a broken circle of tears
The steady pulse of the breathing machine
Counting away the years
The doctor said she can't respond
And it won't be very long
I played a song called Summertime
And her daughter sang along
So spread your wings and take to the sky
And a smile came over her face
She opened her eyes and looked into my soul
With a peaceful, heavenly grace
(She said) Don't cry for me my son cause my life has been good

I wish you well my love and I'd stay here if I could

Don't let the days slip by - live your life till your last breath

And when your time has come you'll go with no regrets

And you'll have a beautiful death

There was a joy in the sadness

A vision of hope and faith

We all got down on our knees

And we began to pray

Spread your wings and take to the sky

And she held my hand so tight

Then she gently let me go

And her smile was a sweet goodbye

Don't cry for me my son cause my life has been good

I wish you well my love and I'd stay here if I could

Don't let the days slip by - live your life till your last breath

And when your time has come you'll go with no regrets

Don't cry for me my son cause my life has been good

I wish you well my love and I'd stay here if I could

Don't let the days slip by - live your life till your last breath

And when your time has come you'll go with no regrets

And you'll have a beautiful death

And you'll have a beautiful death

© 2013 Tom Dalton

(By Music Therapist Tom Dalton)

* * *

146

Ponder and Practice

> Is there a favorite song that you would like to listen to as you exit this world and if so, what is it?

> The most predominant feeling at funerals is not sadness, but *regret*. What are your regrets? What can you do about them today?

> According to this poem, you will have a *beautiful death* "if you'll go with no regrets," and the way to have no regrets is "to *live* your life till your last breath."

51. Amen

It was just another day at the hospice inpatient unit. Brothers, sisters, wives, and husbands needing comfort care filled rooms and two hallways. I walked into the next room and met another dying man—somebody's brother, somebody's son. The room was as cool and dark as the storm outside the window. I pulled a brass chain on a bed lamp and some light broke in. It streaked across the room and lay across the sheet draped form.

"Hi Bill, I'm the chaplain on your care team. I'd like to spend some time with you."

As expected, Bill did not apparently respond. Like so many other patients, he was so weak and so sick he could not respond. "Apparently" is an important qualifier. Many patients still can hear and process words long after they lose the physical ability to speak or move or focus their eyes.

I pulled a chair over, and sat down beside this quiet man, placing a hand on his forearm.

"Hi Bill."

I sat quietly for some time replaying the phone conversation I had shared earlier with Bill's sister. Bill, 57, was the youngest of four siblings, two boys and two girls. He had drifted from the family into trouble many years ago, but they were always there for him. Five years ago, their parents died in a car accident. Since then, Bill had been more or less homeless, and sporadically in contact with the family. During his younger days, he was a fairly successful mechanic. He played football in high school. He never married and had no children, but had many nieces and nephews. He was raised Baptist, but had not been religious for most of his life. The family said that they would be grateful for my prayers.

I gazed into Bill's glassy green, unmoving, eyes. I thought of the tragic events of the night which brought him to the hospice unit. He was found beside a pharmacy, in the parking lot, by friends. He had been at a party that night, drinking heavily, and then "disappeared." Someone remembered him, going to get more beer. It looked like he had fallen and hit his head pretty hard. He was unconscious when they found him. There was brain hemorrhage. There was heroin in his blood. He was trapped: trapped in this dark estranged silence.

"Bill, I want to pray for you. I don't know if you can hear me, but I know a long time ago, you used to attend church, so I want to pray for you."

I bowed my head and thanked God for Bill. I thanked God for his life—for the way his smile made others feel warm, for the way his hands wrapped around a football, for the way he patted a teammate on the back after a great play down the middle. I thanked God for the times he helped his momma around the house, the way he hugged his sister when she was hurt, the way he told jokes with his brother, and the way he made his daddy proud when he fixed the starter on the old Dodge. So much to be grateful for the mystery of this man, I didn't really know.

I bowed my head and shared grief with Bill. There are so many things we both had done wrong, so many things we had left undone, so many ways we had let our family and our God down. We apologized and together asked for God's mercy. I assured Bill he was forgiven.

149

I finished my prayer asking for God's care for Bill, this man no longer such a stranger. "Lord, where there is hurting, bring comfort; where there is fear, bring love; where there is loneliness, bring your company; where there is darkness, bring your light. Amen".

Bill slowly, clearly, mouthed the word, "Amen."

In our meeting as chaplain and patient, God answered that prayer for both of us.

(By Chaplain Steven M. Jurgens-Ling)

* * *

Ponder and Practice

> Begin a conscious practice to say a "five second prayer" for the person you are going to interact with, which will produce an "amen" in his heart, making the interaction easy and graceful.

> Prayer is less about changing the mind of God, and more about transforming our minds to see the purposes of God in our lives, and surrender to them.

> When you pray for others, make it a practice to write the name(s) of the person(s) you are praying for on a piece of paper and hold it in your folded hands and pray...you will be surprised.

52. Kidnapped

Jack is a 79 year old patient on my hospice team. He is diagnosed with Alzheimer's, and lives in the "memory care unit" of an assisted living facility. Martha, his wife of 57 years, lives in an apartment adjacent to the facility. She has Parkinson's disease. Jack was a business major and has worked for prestigious companies. He is currently non-verbal and spends most of his days in bed or in a wheelchair.

Jack's son Matt described his father as a hardworking man, a devout Christian who raised his family in the church. It breaks Matt's heart to see his dad living with no quality of life. It bothers him that his father does not recognize him anymore.

Matt said that he "lost" his father about two years ago when Alzheimer began to set in. One day he made a "scene" while at the bank which was both embarrassing and painful.

They had just pulled up to the drive-thru window of a local bank. When the car stopped, his father opened the door, got out, and ran screaming for help because he thought he was being kidnapped.

Matt went after him into the bank; his father yelled to call the police. The bank employee called the police. Before the police arrived, Jack had left the bank and ran through the parking lot, and had gone into a store. The police cornered him in the store and managed to calm him down. Matt had to prove with his photo ID that he was the son before they would let him take his father home. That was a heart breaking experience for Matt.

Matt has his hands full with the responsibilities of taking care of his ailing father, now under hospice care. But he is also charged with the burdens of taking care of his mother who has Parkinson's.

Martha tells her son that her husband got Alzheimer's because of the stress that she caused him during their marriage. Matt has now the additional burden of dealing with his mother's unmitigated guilt.

I had the pleasure of visiting with Martha, a charming lady, still keeping busy with singing in the choir at the facility and by engaging in other leisure activities. She is worried about her husband. "That's not the husband that I know for 57 years. I wish God would take him out of his misery; it's hard to see him like this. I haven't visited him for two weeks," she said.

When I asked her how her husband being in hospice care has affected her and how she was coping with it, Martha said that she had faith in God which would help her cope. And then she added that she believed in *spiritualism*—the hope that her husband would visit her after he is gone. When I asked her if that was part of her Methodist faith, she said that it was part of her "Hindu belief."

That day I learned about another coping mechanism for loss and grief—the hope of being visited by our loved ones!

(By Chaplain Grellet Sainvilus)

* * *

Ponder and Practice

> Have you had an experience of being "embarrassed" by the behavior of others around you? Describe the experience, share your feelings, and how did you cope?

> Follow the advice of Wayne Dyer to "have a mind that is open to everything and attached to nothing," which will help you learn new things every day.

> If your loved one has Alzheimer's and you want to learn more about dealing with it, check out, **www.alz.org** which offers great resources and information.

53. Spiritual Intimacy

My first few experiences of connecting with the terminally ill came many years before I became a hospice volunteer. In fact, I was embarrassed to admit to the volunteer director that I had felt a special connection with the dying. It felt weird to admit that I was drawn to comforting the terminally ill. She assured me that this type of work was a *calling,* and she encouraged me to look into their volunteer training program.

There were three occasions where I knew deep within that I had to answer this *calling* to become a hospice volunteer. The first was when I spent a few hours with my mother-in-law who was in a partial coma, struggling to breathe. She had been battling cancer for a few years. As I held her hand and prayed, I felt I was assisting her in her transition. It was a privilege to provide her comfort in her last hours.

A few months later, I went to the hospital to visit a woman who was a church member. She had terminal cancer. When I walked in, she was awake but unable to speak, as she had a breathing apparatus covering her nose and mouth. She smiled as if to say, *Thanks for caring enough to stop in.* I remember this incredible power and strength that came over me while sitting at her bedside. As I sat, making eye contact and holding her hands in mine, I felt a profound feeling of what could only be called *spiritual intimacy.* She died a few days later.

The final time this calling came to me was when a good friend was dying from the AIDS virus. During her last days, she wanted only two visitors—her best friend and myself. I felt honored that I would be among her chosen visitors. When I entered her home, I noticed that she was in her pajamas, her hair was disheveled, and she was not wearing any makeup. External appearance didn't seem to matter to her at that moment. It was just two people, raw, vulnerable, and connected at the heart. During my final visit, no words were spoken. I stroked her hair and "told" her without speaking that she was going to be okay and it would be all right if she wanted to let go.

I received a call the next day that she had passed on. As sad as I was, I remember a feeling of deep gratitude coming over me for the gift of spending those final weeks with her as her trusted visitor.

It was few weeks after that I walked into the hospice office to inquire about becoming a volunteer. After hearing my stories, the volunteer director was convinced that I had a *calling* to be a hospice volunteer. I attended a two-day training. As the weekend progressed, I too knew without a doubt that this was the calling for me and that I was ready to go.

Few weeks after my training, I was assigned the first patient. I was not ready as I had thought, because my first patient was a six-month old terminally ill baby girl. Her Mom was looking for a few respite hours a week. My job was to hold the little girl for 3 or 4 hours a day, mostly watching her sleep. As I held her in my arms, gently rocking her, my heart connected with this little girl—as I prayed for healing and comfort for her. It has been years since that experience, but I have never forgotten about that little girl who deeply touched my life.

Another case that comes to mind is that of an elderly male patient in a nursing home. During the first visit, we connected. I remember bringing special music to play in his room. We would sit together and listen to soft meditation music which was soothing to his spirit. He also loved to go outside in his wheelchair, often wanting to just sit next to my motorcycle. When the call finally came that my friend had passed, once again, I felt an extreme sense of gratitude for sharing his life with me during his final days.

I now know that hospice work is indeed a calling. Many wonder how anyone would want to do this work. It is not something I planned to do. I see it as a gift and a blessing to share the kind of intimacy that goes deeper than anything I have ever known.

I often wonder what would be like if I were to become a patient myself—being at the receiving end of hospice care.

It is comforting to know that I will be definitely—in good hands.

(By Jack Bloomfield, Hospice Volunteer)

* * *

Ponder and Practice

> Everybody has a "calling." Have you discovered yours?

> Erase the notion that you *have* a soul, and believe that you *are* a soul. That change in consciousness, could change everything— your identity, your purpose, your life itself.

> "Volunteers are the only human beings on the face of the earth who reflect this nation's compassion, unselfish caring, patience, and just plain loving one another." ~Erma Bombeck

54. Eulogy Virtues

In his book, *The Road to Character*, New York Times columnist and conservative pundit David Brooks, talks about "resume virtues" and "eulogy virtues."

Resume virtues are the ones you list on your resume, the skills that you bring to the job market that contribute to external success. The eulogy virtues have a different focus, and are deeper. They are the virtues that get talked about at your funeral, the ones that exist at the core of your being—whether or not you are kind, brave, honest and faithful; what kind of relationships you formed and the difference you made in life.

Most of us think that eulogy virtues are more important than resume virtues, but we rarely act on cultivating them. The author confesses that he has not focused on eulogy virtues for most of his life which brings me to the story of Walter.

Walter was a patient on my hospice team. He was only 62 years old. When I visited him for the first time, I saw a healthy looking, handsome man sitting in a wheelchair. He had a blank stare, and had no ability to speak. My first reaction was a moment of *transference*—the eerie feeling that it could be me sitting in that chair, and I am older than Walter. I was anxious to find out what caused him to be under hospice care at such a young age.

Walter was a successful businessman with celebrity connections, and he had built up a business empire. According to his sister, Walter worked six days a week, 12 hour days, and did not take vacations. He was so consumed by his work that when she called him, he was too busy to even talk to her. He would end the conversation by saying: "I have to get back to work."

Walter was married for a few years but the marriage ended in divorce, as he had no time to nurture the relationship. His wife got a divorce and obtained custody of their only son. His son, now 32 years old, has not visited his father in the past 15 years.

Walter was so busy with work that he neglected his health. He did not have the time or the inclination to get medical check-ups. Two months before his 62nd birthday, Walter had a massive stroke that left him partially paralyzed and speechless. Now he lives in an assisted living facility under hospice care.

Walter's sister is angry at him for not taking care of his health. She is mad that he was a workaholic and did not find time for his wife or son. It breaks her heart to see her baby brother, who used to hobnob with the rich and the famous, now confined to the lonely environment of an elder care facility. He is at the mercy of a home health aide who will change his diapers three times a day, feed him three meals a day, and push him around in a wheelchair from the living room to the bed room and back.

At the end of the visit when I prayed with Walter for his peace and comfort, I was saddened by the fact that most people continue to focus on resume virtues rather than eulogy virtues during their life time. Walter's story is yet another reminder for me to re-focus my energies to cultivate eulogy virtues.

* * *

Ponder and Practice

> We *exist* in a *three* dimensional world (*four* if we include time), but we are called to *live* at the minimum, in a *five* dimensional universe. That fifth dimension is the *spiritual* dimension. Do you spend any time in that dimension on a daily basis? How?

> There are 168 hours a week. Would you consider spending one of those hours in a faith community to increase your odds, by at least 50 percent, of being a more peaceful and joyful person? The return on this investment could be *huge!*

> Do a thirty-minute fantasy meditation listening to *your* eulogy. Who is giving it and what is s/he saying, and how does it make you feel?

157

55. Love Handles

For a split seismic second, my soon-to-be Medicare-age male ego fluttered, flushed, and felt faintly flattered—and flattened fast. I knew that the bikini-clad pictures the woman was texting me were not meant for me. It was an electronic error of a grieving widow who felt moribund and mortified about sending them to the priest, who had officiated the memorial service for her husband two days earlier.

Jenny's husband Jerry was 50 years old when he died of liver cancer. She honored him with a memorial service on a Saturday afternoon. On Sunday morning, I received a text from Jenny: "Thank you so much Pastor Paul, for the service for my husband. It was spiritual and touching; Jerry would have liked it."

And I texted back: "Thank you, Jenny. Glad to be able to help. I pray that God and Jerry's angel help you move forward." That was it. I had moved forward.

The next day I received two photos of Jenny in a bikini with a message in Spanish: *Tengo q bajar los gorditos, jijiji.* My Spanish-ignorant brain thought it was something naughty.

Instantly, I showed the text and the pictures to my wife Judy, because I had nothing to hide. It is always a safe thing to do, to prove your innocence and maintain marital peace. Judy looked up the Spanish dictionary to find out the meaning of the message. It was innocent. (*I have to lose my love-handles, hahaha*). Jenny was talking about getting rid of her love handles. I had a sigh of relief, especially for Jenny's sake.

Just as I had suspected, it was a misdirected text. While we were looking up the Spanish dictionary, my phone rang. It was Jenny. Her voice was quivering. She apologized profusely for sending those pictures to me. I allayed her anxiety and told her:

"Don't worry about it; this happens all the time; it was an innocent mistake; don't be too hard on yourself; I deleted them; be at peace."

I told her about my *faux pas,* once sending a text message to my female boss: *Will pick you up after work and let us go for dinner first and for shopping later.* Of course, it was meant for my wife, but in my hurried, not-paying-attention mode, I sent it to my boss. We both laughed about our embarrassing electronic errors. Jenny was relieved that I didn't mishandle the situation.

Jenny had texted the pictures to her girlfriend, inviting her to go to the pool to exercise so that she could get rid of her love handles. Since she didn't hear back from her friend for hours, Jenny wondered if she hadn't gotten the message. So Jenny went back to her phone and checked, and she almost fainted when she realized that the text was mistakenly sent to me. She told me that she was sweating bullets before calling me. She was embarrassed and ashamed about sending her pictures in beach attire to a priest, especially the priest who had just officiated at the memorial service for her husband.

The Information Super Highway is a good place to travel. It takes you to your destinations easily and fast. But, like any speed-way, wrecks are common and some of them can be deadly. Jenny's was not.

It is always a good policy not to send any pictures to anybody unless it is a picture that you don't mind the public to see. We also need to be extremely careful about what we write in our texts and emails. Unlike a message on a paper which we can go back and correct or even erase, electronic transmissions, once the "send" button is clicked, are beyond your control. The unintended consequences of a hurried message or an image sent carelessly or in anger can be unpredictable, and sometimes, even dangerous.

* * *

Ponder and Practice

> Have you had an experience like Jenny's in your life? What did you sent and to whom? How did that turn out?

> Make it a habit to take that extra-second to double-check the address/phone number of the person you are sending a message to. Also practice taking a deep breath, before you say anything to anyone.

> Practice *mindful living* as opposed to *mere meandering*. Spend 15 minutes a day for meditation. Check out ***www. mindful.org*** to learn about mindfulness, and how it can enhance all areas of your life.

56. Facing Grief

In my grief support group, I meet some individuals who go through intense grief at the loss of their loved ones. I also have the privilege of seeing them coming out of their grief in one piece and moving forward, having used the experience for greater living. One such individual, Bill, who grieved deeply for his lover, shared with the group his own thoughts and three other quotes which can help anyone "walking through the valley of the shadow of death." Here they are:

As my intense grief surrounding Kathy's death begins to fade slowly, and the very hard edges of the pain ever so slightly begin to soften, I know that I will eventually weigh anchor and catch the wind (carpe ventus) on a phantom sailboat I shall name "Kathy Forevermore." As I come about and set the main sail to catch the full force of the wind, as it blows in another direction and is always shifting, I navigate toward my future of calm seas, turbulent waters, and unforeseen storms ahead. Though my first mate is not on deck with me, I am calm with her in my heart. Steady as she goes!

~ William J. Kieffer

In this sad world of ours, sorrow comes to all, and it often comes with bitter agony. Perfect relief is not possible, except with time. You cannot now believe that you will ever feel better, but that is not true. You are sure to be happy again. Knowing this, truly believing it, will make you less miserable now. I have had enough experience to make this statement.

~Abraham Lincoln

Grief can destroy you—or focus you. You can decide a relationship was all for nothing if it had to end in death and you are alone. Or you can realize that every moment of it had more meaning than you dared to recognize at the time, so much meaning it scared you, so you just lived, just took for granted the love and laughter of each day, and didn't allow yourself to consider the sacredness of it. But when it's over and you're alone, you begin to see that it wasn't just a movie and a dinner together, not just watching sunsets together, not just scrubbing a floor or washing dishes together or worrying over a high electric bill. It was everything, it was the way of life, every event and precious moment of it. The answer to the mystery of existence is the love you shared sometimes so imperfectly, and when the loss wakes you to the deeper beauty of it, to the sanctity of it, you can't get off your knees for a long time. You're driven to your knees not by the weight of the loss but by gratitude for what preceded the loss. And the ache is always there, but one day not the emptiness, because to nurture the emptiness, to take solace in it, is to disrespect the gift of life.

~Dean Koontz, *Odd Hours*

If ever there is a tomorrow when we're not together

There is something you must always remember.

You are braver than you believe, stronger than you seem, and smarter than you think.

But the most important thing is, even if we are apart, I'll always be with you.

~Winnie the Pooh

* * *

Ponder and Practice

> "Talk" with the person who died. During moments of solitude, talk to the person you lost as if s/he were right there with you. Say whatever is on your mind, everything you wished you had said while s/he was still alive. Take a few moments to feel a sense of peace.

> Use your imagination and write a letter *from* your loved one, mail it to your address, and read it when you miss him/her the most.

> Do a favorite activity of the person who died on their birthday and/or on the anniversary of their death such as watching a favorite movie, visiting a favorite place, listening to a favorite song or eating a favorite meal

57. Why Me?

Six months after the death of her 96 year old mother, Jane started attending my bereavement support group. She wanted to "deal with the pain of loss of my mother and best friend." Week after week, Jane talked about what a wonderful mother she has had and how "unfair" it was for God to take her away from her.

Using the word "unfair" about the loss of a parent who lived to the ripe age of 96 is unfair. I noticed other participants rolling their eyes when Jane used the word "unfair" to describe her experience. Being a professional, I only rolled my mental eyes. Jane was obviously suffering from the "why me" syndrome which is often rampant in bereavement support groups.

One day, when Jane was marching along on her self-pity parade, Nancy spoke up. She was a 48 year old woman who had lost her only son to suicide. Now, that could be an "unfair" deal, and she may have a legitimate right to ask the "Why me?" question. But Nancy surprised us all when she began to speak.

This is the gist of what she said:

Forgive me for saying this, but as sad and angry and depressed and desolate as I am, I don't ask, "Why me?" because, when I ask that question, it sounds like I wish it was somebody else in my place. I don't wish my plight on anyone else. It is a horrible place and I don't wish any parent to go through that lonely road of tragedy and tears. Instead, I ask the question: "Why not me?" which brings a sense of peace to my heart.

I was inspired by Nancy's words. I could not believe my ears that a young woman who had lost her only son to a tragic loss could speak the words she did.

All of us have asked that un-answerable question at some time in our lives. I stopped asking it a long time ago. Instead, like Nancy, I ask *Why not me?*

First of all, *Why me?* is an unproductive question. There is no verifiable and acceptable answer to that question. Humans have tried to answer it with platitudes and clichés like: "It must be God's will," "God wanted him more than we did," "He is in a better place," etc. Be patient with those who offer such answers. They mean well. It is their way of coping with the paradox of life.

Second, *Why me?* is triggered by a lack of appreciation for the mystery of life. Many experiences in life defy explanation, and are devoid of answers. *Life happens,* and the best way to cope with the twists and turns of our life journey is to go with the flow and align with the impulses of the universe of which we are an integral part.

Third, *Why me?* is a "victim question," prompted by feelings of helplessness and hopelessness, wondering *why God is picking on me?* A new understanding of God might help us not to ask that question or at least rephrase it.

Fourth, *Why me?* originates from a sense of *entitlement,* that life owes us certain things, that we are entitled to a certain number of years, and that we *deserve* a happy, healthy, trouble-free life. Life offers no such guarantees. Most things in life have warranties, but life itself has no warranties. None of us are *entitled* but all of us are *endowed.* We are endowed with a brain, if we care to use it; we are endowed with the *divine image,* if we choose to acknowledge it, and activate it; we are blessed with gifts and talents, if we decide to use them.

When we live with expectations and a sense of entitlement, every little disappointment becomes a tragedy. Every sad experience begets bitterness. We forget that *loss is the law o life!* Joy dries up in our hearts, and smile fades from our face.

I encourage you to delete the word *entitlement* from the dictionary of your life, and replace it with the word *gratitude,* and watch what happens. You will be in for a magic carpet ride!

* * *

165

Ponder and Practice

> Why is it that we don't ask "Why me?" when nice things happen to us? I have never heard any one ask: "Why me winning this lottery?" "Why me getting this promotion?" "Why me having good health?"

> For most people, "negative bias" is their default approach to life. Make "positive bias" your default approach by focusing on the blessings rather than the concerns in your life.

> There are about 105,000 flights a day in the world. When they are all safe, we don't hear about them. But one plane-crash makes the news. Regardless of our circumstances, *blessings/concerns* ratio in our lives is usually, 90/10, but we behave as if it is 10/90. Consciously practice "positive bias" on a daily basis.

58. Dating While Married

Is it wrong to date while being married? I asked.

Most of my colleagues answered it in the affirmative: "Yes, it is wrong." "It is okay if your wife gives you permission," said one persons jokingly.

My answer: "It depends."

I was prompted to ask this question during a conference on Alzheimer's disease titled, *The Longest Loss*. The speakers talked about the mental and emotional pain this long, drawn out disease causes both for the patient and the caregivers, especially for the caregivers. A book called *The 36-hour Day* by Nancy Mace and Peter Rabins is an apt title for a book about Alzheimer's.

My answer demands more data. So here it is:

Jim and Jill are residents of an Alzheimer's unit. There are about twenty patients in that unit. Both Jim and Jill have advanced Alzheimer's. They are mostly bed ridden, and non-verbal.

Jim and Jill have devoted spouses. Jim's wife, Maria visits three to four times a week. She also attends the support group for spouses on Thursdays. They have been married for 54 years. Maria grieves the loss of her amazing husband to this "wretched disease." Their plan of retiring together and traveling were all dashed. She feels like a crypto-widow among her couple friends, because her husband is "dead," but not exactly. After every visit, she returns with an aching heart to an empty house.

Jill's husband, Matt is also a very devoted spouse. They have been married for 57 years. Jill had an early diagnosis of Alzheimer's at age 63. Matt took care of his wife in the house with assistance from an aide for ten years before placing her in the assisted living facility. He visited daily, sat next to Jill holding her hands, occasionally straightening out a stray hair on her forehead. He would talk to her tenderly, stroke her hair gently, and whisper, "I love you, honey" into her ear, before the parting kiss. Matt always talked about the wonderful life they had before the disease struck her.

Maria's and Matt's paths crossed several times while they were visiting their spouses. They also attended the same support group. They were experiencing the same loss; they were fighting the same enemy; they were undergoing the same crisis; they spoke the same language; they felt the same pain; they were on the same ground; they traveled the same road; they swam in the same emotional ocean; and they were in the same boat!

Their agonizing stories of loss and pain brought them together. They went out for coffee together; then it was dinner together, followed by long walks on the beach two miles away from the facility where their respective spouses lived.

Matt was a realist. He talked about his wife being no more present in Jill. "She is existing, not living," he told me once. He must have been rationalizing to assuage any sense of guilt he might have had for being closer to another woman while his wife was still alive.

Maria too had her moments of guilt, but she assuaged them by thinking that if the shoe were on the other foot, her husband would not have behaved any differently than what she was doing now.

On September 18, 2008, Maria's husband Jim died. I officiated at the funeral. Matt was at the funeral comforting Maria. Matt's wife died the same year on December 3rd. She was cremated. I had the privilege of doing a memorial service for her in the club house at Matt's condo.

A few months after the death of their respective spouses, Maria moved into Matt's condo.

In January 2011, I received a phone call from Matt. "Guess what chaplain Paul, Maria and I are getting married, and we want you to marry us. You know our story more than anyone we can think of."

I was delighted that two souls had found each other again…that their common pain had brought them together and their

168

lives—what is left of it—does not have to be lived in isolation and loneliness.

On March 8, 2011, I blessed the marriage of Matt and Maria near the Deerfield Beach Pier, surrounded by their immediate family.

Matt was 82 and Maria was 78. While signing their marriage license, Matt and Maria might have been signing a new lease on their lives—and seeing the light of love again, at the end of the dark tunnel of sadness and loss.

I think "it depends" is a good phrase to remember when faced with the quandaries and mysteries of life.

* * *

Ponder and Practice

> Avoid binary thinking—yes/no, either/or, black/white, and appreciate the irony, paradox, complexity, and mystery of life.

> Nothing in life should be written on stones. Stone-writing belongs in graveyards. Erase *absolutes* from your life, and embrace *relativity.*

> *If You Meet the Buddha on the Road, Kill Him,* is the title of a book. What does that mean? Explore. Read the book. It could change your thinking about life.

59. Finding Love Again

What are your thoughts on post-death dating and marriage by a surviving spouse?

"Positive" was my one-word answer to Sam who posed that question during a meeting of our weekly bereavement support group. I later found out that Sam wanted to get the group's thoughts because he was grappling with an issue that many widows and widowers wrestle with.

While a minority in the group was not in favor of the idea of dating and remarrying at all, the majority viewed it as an "it depends" question. Several factors are at play when considering such a sensitive topic. Age, health, length and strength of the previous marriage, psychological disposition, and financial situation are a few of the important factors that affect the dating needs, and outcomes of grieving spouses. If you add minor children into the mix, it can be a very complicated situation.

One of the objections raised against re-marriage was the issue of guilt. Some thought that the deceased spouse would be jealous or unhappy if the surviving spouse hooked up with another person. This unnecessary guilt has prevented many people from finding happiness in their lives after the death of a loved one. I believe that jealousy and possessiveness are above-the-grave feelings. We have them during our existence on this side of the grave. After death, when our loved ones turn into angels, they are beyond human feelings that mess up many relationships. I believe that a departed spouse, who is presumably in heaven, would be delighted to see his or her surviving partner living a heavenly life on earth.

I was pleasantly surprised when a friend of mine, who is a nurse, agreed with me on this point. This is perhaps the only point we agree on, considering that this particular nurse is extremely conservative in her views about everything else in life. She is the wife of a pastor, and a biblical literalist. But when it comes to remarriage after the death of a spouse, she was extremely liberal. Her argument was simple and straightforward:

"I made a promise to God that I will be faithful to my husband *until death do us part*...now that death has taken him away, I am free to re-marry if I choose to; whether I want to is a different question." While there is no cookie cutter solution to fit all scenarios, if one can find the ideal person, it can be a blessing for both. Sam who raised the issue in the group and Sally who was a participant in the same group—were two such individuals.

Both were in their early seventies. Sam's wife had died after a long battle with breast cancer, and Sally's husband had died of heart disease. They listened to each other's stories in the context of the bereavement support group. Sam felt drawn to Sally and after being in the group for about six months, Sam invited Sally out for dinner. They went to the *Olive Garden* restaurant, had a great dinner and talked for another two hours after dinner.

Two months after "graduating" from the bereavement group, they returned to the group together. There were about fifteen grieving spouses in the group that day. Sam and Sally were all smiles and they had come to announce that they were engaged. When they saw the mood of the group—a predictable scene of sorrow and sadness—they held back. They thought it would be inappropriate to show their mirth in the midst of death.

Few months later, I received a call from Sam requesting me to bless their marriage. Again, I was delighted to participate in a special moment of their life-journey, of which I was a part at a critical time.

They wanted to make their wedding memorable by getting married on a special day. So, on 10/10/10, I blessed the marriage of Sam and Sally at an Italian restaurant in Fort Lauderdale.

It was a simple ceremony attended by close family and friends. The children of Sam and Sally shed tears of joy because their parents had found love again.

* * *

Ponder and Practice

> What are your thoughts on re-marriage after the death of a spouse? How would you assuage the guilt of someone struggling with this issue?

> If you had an opportunity to start over and marry again, would you choose your current spouse as your partner again?

> Make a list of truths/things that you consider "absolutes" in your life. How many do you have? If I were to say that number should be "zero," what would you say?

60. The Skinny Little Girl

My Monday evening grief support group had just started. The six participants that day, all in their early seventies had lost their loved ones, and had come to find support and comradarie. Then a skinny little girl walked in, and everyone wondered why she was coming to our group.

Her name was Amanda. She was a high-school student who chose to do her school project on grief support groups, and she had come to observe our group. The group was not too inclined to have a teenager with them listening to their stories. As moderator, I felt that she should have inquired first before showing up to a place where emotions are laid bare.

Noticing our hesitation, Amanda said: "I am grieving too," and before anyone had a chance to ask about her loss, she blurted out: "I had an abortion," and burst into tears. The woman next to her, put her arms around Amanda and comforted her.

The dynamics of the group instantly changed. My heart broke for the little girl sitting in front of me, visibly shaken and broken. Her deep sigh penetrated the eerie silence of the room, and her tears fell on the carpet floor and disappeared.

Amanda was 17 and her boyfriend 16. When he found out that his girl friend was pregnant, he wanted to bail. He told her that if she decided to keep the baby, he would leave her. His parents had told him that if he made a girl pregnant, he would be disowned by them. Amanda and her boy friend were terrified about their parents finding out, the potential baby ruining their future, and the sheer magnitude of problems ahead.

Florida State law requires that minors seeking an abortion must at least inform one of their parents about their decision to get an abortion. Some States require a parent to give "informed consent" allowing the abortion. If no parent consents, the minor may be able to get a "judicial bypass" from the court.

To obtain a judicial bypass, the minor must file an application at the county court. The judge will consider a variety of factors, including whether or not the minor is mature enough to give informed consent, whether or not she is emancipated, and if an abortion is in the best interests of the minor.

Amanda being terrified of her parents' reaction, went before a county judge and secured a judicial bypass. Her boyfriend drove her to the courthouse and waited outside. He also drove her to the clinic, paid for the procedure, and drove her home.

In an ideal world, no child should go through the nightmare Amanda had experienced. But we live in an imperfect world. My heart went out to that hurting child with empathy and compassion, and I offered to help her through this difficult time. Amanda did not have the resources to pay a therapist.

Amanda never returned to the group. She did not seek counseling from me either. The Amandas of the world create *blessed unrest* in my heart.

* * *

Ponder and Practice

> Expand your definition of *loss* and make a list of losses a human being has to face from birth to death.

> What are your thoughts on abortion?

> Some of the staunchest *pro-life* proponents are *pro-gun, pro-death penalty,* and *pro-war.* How do you explain that?

61. S**t Happens

Once I was asked to substitute for a grief support group moderator who suddenly fell ill. The group was in an assisted living facility. There were nine participants ranging in age from 77 to 102. Five of them arrived using their walkers. One of them had to stop and rest several times on the way to the room through the long corridors of the building, because he had a mild case of COPD. Three of them were wheeled in by their aides. One arrived on a motorized scooter.

Sitting in front of me were nine individuals with a combined life experience of 746 years. If their life stories were to be told, it would take the rest of their lives to complete them and nobody would get out of that room alive. We had just one hour for the group session. Only five of the nine participants were able to engage in meaningful conversation.

Most of them attend these groups not necessarily with any special goal in mind but as "something to do" during the day, while living "boring and monotonous" lives in the predictable environment of an assisted living facility. Most residents don't keep track of the days or dates because "they are all the same."

While three of the participants sat in their wheelchairs and slept through most of the session, six of them talked—mostly whining and complaining except for one person—Jimmy.

Sarah, 87, sat with a sour face most of the time, but when she spoke, she had a litany of complaints about her daughter who "never visits me." *She lives in New Jersey and comes to see me only once a*

*year. I am so mad I should have had more than one child. If I had a
few more children, may be one of them would have visited me often.*

Edna's issue was not about uncaring children. She is 93 years
old. Her son and daughter who live nearby, regularly visit and
sometimes take her out for lunch. She is very upset that her sister
died recently. She was very close to her sister who lived on the
second floor of the same facility. She died at the age of 95. Edna is
so angry about it because "there was nothing wrong with her."

Leon who spoke up next was 89. He was a mailman in
Brooklyn, and retired to Florida two decades ago. He complained
about the "tasteless food" he had to eat every day at "this lousy
place." He is not a happy camper. *There is nothing to do here; I
can't go anywhere because my kids took away my driver's license
and sold my car.* He is upset that his hearing is bad and his kids
won't replace the hearing aids. By the way, he lost two sets of
hearing aids before his son decided not to spend money on them
again. He told his dad: "Dad, the less you hear, the better."

After listening to mostly whining and complaining, my
attention turned to Jimmy who seemed to be pensive and quiet. He
was the youngest of the group—63 years old. He was the one who
arrived on a motor scooter. He sat with his head bent to the side,
drooling slightly while his hands shook mildly. Jimmy was
diagnosed with Parkinson's disease at the age of 52! He lived in the
house with his wife until few years ago with the assistance of an
aide. When it became financially unfeasible, his wife placed him at
the assisted living facility.

Considering his age and the discomfort of his disability,
Jimmy should have been the saddest and the angriest person in the
room. Surprisingly, he was the most optimistic and cheerful of the
bunch. So, I was curious to hear about his coping strategy in an
apparently hopeless situation.

Jimmy was a man of few words. But the two cryptic words
he uttered that morning have always stuck in my memory.

With a stoic look and in a casual tone he said: "Shit
happens."

176

Life is full of unpredictable events. *Cest la vie* is a less pungent expression of the same idea. The phrase is an acknowledgment that bad things happen to people for no particular reason. The slang "shit happens" allegedly has its origin in the movie, *Forrest Gump.*

When he was running across the country, a bumper sticker designer asked him to say something that could be put on a bumper sticker. At that time, Forrest stepped on some dog excrement, and the guy said to him "Whoa! man, you just ran through a big pile of dog shit!" Then Gump said, "It happens," and the guy asked: "What? Shit?" and Gump replied: "Sometimes."

Ironically, Jimmy had a Gump-ish demeanor and drawl. He didn't bother to list a litany of complaints about his bad luck in life. He didn't whine about his wife placing him in a facility. He couldn't care less if fellow residents pitied or praised him. He was not upset about the hassles of navigating his scooter through the narrow corridors of the building.

Jimmy was not a member of any organized religion. He didn't think much about God. "I am a realist," he said, and "there are lot of things in life beyond my control and whining about it is not going to change anything."

"I think I had a good life, as bad as it was," he added.

Jimmy seemed to have no sympathy for those who stubbornly refused to let the past go. He had no patience for those who were insisting on marinating in their misery.

In difficult moments of life, I delve into my psycho-spiritual tool-kit for coping strategies. I have a variety of tools in there—faith in God, trusting the process and hoping that everything will turn out okay in the long run. But of late, I have come to experience the effectiveness of Jimmy's strategy in a lot of situations.

Life is hard. Nothing is guaranteed. Be grateful for what you have and yes, *shit happens.*

Words of Author Scott Lynch can be helpful in this context:

Life boils down to standing in line to get shit dropped on your head. Everyone's got a place in the queue, you can't get out of it, and just when you start to congratulate yourself on surviving your dose of shit, you discover that the line is actually circular.

* * *

Ponder and Practice

> The landscape of life is riddled with landmines and diamonds. Maturity means, in the words of Jack Gilbert "having the stubbornness to accept our gladness in the ruthless furnace of this world."

> Refuse to be lobotomized by society. Stop looking for answers from the wizard behind the curtain. Instead, wake up the wizard within you.

> Remember that stress is not purchased at the supermarket, but manufactured in your mind. Flush your mind with "meditation fluid" and throw away the medication bottles!

62. Acceptance

When Jane walked into the support group, she was a basket case of emotions—anger, denial, sadness, and depression. Her sullen face and sunken eyes revealed a hurting heart. She sat quietly listening to the stories of other participants and barely talked despite encouragement from me and others. Tears flowed down her cheek as she heard stories of loss and grief.

Finally, she was ready to talk. She had lost her husband of 52 years after an illness of six months. *We were best friends; we did everything together; he was a devoted husband and father; my children are devastated; he took such good care of me so that I never even learned to drive; today I had to depend on my neighbor to bring me to this group.*

Jane didn't believe in support groups. She thought she had to deal with her grief in her own way. She didn't think others would understand her grief or would be able to help her. She spent her days inside the house, crying. Most days she wouldn't even wake up until noon or change her pajamas. Jane had no energy to do anything.

Her main outlet for her grief was to talk to her two children who lived in nearby towns. In the beginning, the children were sympathetic to their mother, but after many months of unmitigated grief, they lost patience. *They get annoyed when I call them. My son told me to get over it. He can say that, because he has his wife and children, but I have nobody,* said Jane.

Jane's daughter realized that her mom's grief was becoming complicated, because months after the death, mom was grieving "as if it happened yesterday." She was concerned about her mother and convinced her to seek outside help, such as attending a grief support group.

The members of the group were very supportive and sympathetic to Jane. But after several weeks of listening to the litany of her complaints, I noticed that they too were running out of patience for Jane's plight. She seemed to have no insight into the realities of life or the willingness to listen to what others were telling her. Jane was totally focused on her loss.

While talking about how forlorn and forsaken she feels and how unfair and unbearable her situation is, Jane said: *This is terrible; I cannot accept this.*

Jane's statement gave me an opening to talk about acceptance that day. I usually spent the last fifteen minutes for grief education, because I believe that along with the sharing of feelings, there should be an examination of the thinking that generates those feelings. Feelings devoid of thinking are like kites without strings.

So I talked about the five stages of grief from Elizabeth Kubler-Ross—denial, anger, bargaining, depression, and acceptance. I told them that it is not a linear journey but a circular process—there is always the chance of feeling a level of acceptance one day, and suddenly feeling anger all over again.

The pathway to acceptance is a winding road of twists and turns filled with potholes of guilt, shame, regret, and a whole lot of mixed emotions.

Many in the group had reached some level of acceptance. Some had accepted their loss but still had remnants of anger. Others had accepted with a sense of resignation, because they felt helpless to do anything about the situation. A few had accepted their loss with a sense of gratitude. They were grateful for the time they had with their loved ones rather than the time they didn't.

Acceptance with gratitude is an acceptable goal. On that day, I floated the idea of accepting the death of a loved one with *enthusiasm.*

The group members stared at me with this "you-must-be-kidding" look.

I have to accept the death of my husband because I have no choice, and you are telling me I have to accept it with enthusiasm?

That is outrageous. I can accept news of winning lottery with enthusiasm, but not death, said Jane. Others chimed in with similar sentiments.

I told them that when they understood the real meaning of the word *enthusiasm,* they would realize that the best way to deal with loss is to accept it with enthusiasm.

They were all ears, albeit skeptical ears.

The word "enthusiasm" is a combination of *en* (in) and *theos* (god) which means—*in God* or *be possessed by God.*

When I am experiencing deep sorrow, and being confronted by the unexplainable conundrums of life and death, I have no place to go to but God.

My understanding of God as Good Shepherd, who is with me, *even though I walk through the shadow of the valley of death,* brings me solace. My experience of God as *part* of me rather than *apart* from me, brings me peace. My notion of God as a *participant* in my suffering rather than the *perpetrator* of it, brings me comfort.

When I accept my loss in Him, through Him, and with Him, I finally get a glimpse of the deeper meaning of phrases like "winning by losing" and "rising by dying."

* * *

Ponder and Practice

> "Life is a *tragedy* for those who *feel,* and a *comedy* for those who *think.*" Use these words of Horace Wolpe to examine the thinking behind your feelings.

> "I have learned to offer no resistance to what is; I have learned to allow the present moment to be, and to accept the impermanent nature of all things and conditions. Thus I have found peace." ~Eckhart Tolle

> Repeat this prayer often: "God, give me the serenity to accept the things I cannot change, the courage to change the things I can, and the *wisdom* to know the difference."

63. Still with Us

I facilitate a bereavement support group in a county hospital. A group of eight to ten people gather every week to talk about their grief and loss, to offer support to each other, and to receive comfort in that process. I always encourage them to believe that our loved ones have not "gone anywhere," but rather they are still with us *as spirits*, not *in spirit.* There is a big difference.

Being present *in spirit,* means mostly as a memory. Being present a*s spirit* means, a *palpable presence* neither accessible to touch, audible to the ear, nor visible to the eye, but tangible to the soul. Most participants are open to this idea, but there are skeptics too. One such skeptic was Andrea, who had lost her mother on March 17, 2009.

During our meeting on November 30, 2009, Andrea came in with an envelope in her hand, and asked me to open and read the card in it. It was a wedding anniversary card from her mother that had arrived in the mail, on Saturday, November 28, 2009, for Andrea and her husband. And it said: "Dear Andrea and Lee, Happy Anniversary, mom and dad."

November 30th is Andrea's wedding anniversary!
Andrea said that she had received anniversary cards from her mom and dad every year since her marriage. She was sad that she wouldn't receive one this year, as her mother had passed in March, but she did! It was signed by her mom and the address on the envelope was also written by her mom!

The envelope was POST MARKED *November 27, 2008!* Where was that card for a whole year? Why was it not delivered the day after it was posted? Why didn't it show up six months earlier or six months later? Why was it not lost permanently? Why would it arrive on the exact weekend of her anniversary? I told Andrea that it was her mother wishing her a Happy Anniversary. Andrea began to cry. She said she cried for hours when she received the card on Saturday, and was confused, mesmerized, and mystified by it.

Annie's story is similar. After her husband Bud died, she felt alone and lonely. Bud was the love of her life. He was adored by his grandchildren who used to call him "Bachigaloop." Annie thought that a dog would help her ease her loneliness and soothe her pain. She searched on-line for a dog and was instantly attracted to a rescue dog; she made a phone call, and brought the dog home within three days. Guess what the name of that dog is—*Bachi!* Annie thought that Bud was helping her from "beyond" to ease the pain of loss. Annie said that the dog is exactly like her husband—sweet, loving, and has a big mouth. A day after he was brought home, he jumped into bed with her!

My pastor Craig's mom died on August 2, 2015. Two days after her death, Craig and his two sisters went out for lunch to a local diner in Detroit. As usual, Craig ordered a diet coke. Craig had a smile on his face when he saw the word on his coke-can: MOM.

Coca-Cola's *Share-a-Coke* campaign has bottles with thousands of popular names, and for celebratory moments like Mother's Day, Fathers' Day, Weddings, Graduations, Proms and Family re-unions. For example, 8-oz. glass bottles have "Mom," "Dad," "Grad," "Soul mate," and "Hero."

From millions of coke bottles with thousands of names on them, how did Pastor Craig get a bottle with MOM on it during his first visit to a restaurant after his mother's death?

Looks like their mom wanted to join her children for lunch!

I think we should extricate ourselves from the traditional notion that our loved ones have gone to a far away location after their death. We should also delete from our minds the hope of meeting them in the *future,* because, in the spiritual realm, there is neither past nor future but only eternal now. Our loved ones live with us in the *now*, in a different dimension. To the extent that we are able to believe that, and tune in the antenna of our faith in that direction, we will enjoy the company of our loved ones at unpredictable times through unbelievable channels.

* * *

Ponder and Practice

> How does the existence of your loved ones *as spirits* as opposed to *in spirit* change your thinking about them, and your relationship to them?

> What do you think about the experiences Andrea, Annie and Craig had about their loved ones? Have you had similar experiences?

> We live mostly in a three-dimensional world, four if we count time. But according to *String Theory*, there are *ten* dimensions to this universe. How does that awareness change your ideas about your loved ones?

64. Synchronicity

Synchronicity is defined as a series of events or happenings that occur together to make something happen that was thought to be impossible. Some people call it mere coincidence, but I prefer to call it *Godincidence.*

I have experienced it many times in my life, especially in hospice work. I believe that these happenings are orchestrated by the *spirit* of the deceased who has the power to influence events on earth, sometimes to work through unfinished business or to help the living.

A beautiful experience of synchronicity occurred during a death visit years ago. First of all, I was not supposed to be at this house because my team nurse was already there. Since she had to leave for another appointment, I was called in.

Jean died at noon on her birthday, at age 72. She was a widow with no children of her own. Her immediate family consisted of her 80 year old sister, two nephews and two nieces; none of whom were present when their favorite aunt took her last breath.

As they walked into the house to view the body and pay their respects, they burst into tears. I comforted them, prayed with them, and offered solace. The nieces and nephews talked about what a wonderful aunt they had who raised them as her own children.

While discussing funeral arrangements, the patient's nephew expressed the family's intention to cremate the body. The funeral home was called. While waiting for the removal service, the nieces said that their aunt had always wanted to donate her body to medical science to find a cure for cancer. They had discussed it several times, made phone calls to the University of Miami Medical School, but they never got a chance to sign the necessary papers. They felt guilty for not being able to fulfill their aunt's wishes and reluctantly agreed to cremate her body.

It was about 3 p.m. One of the nephews picked up an envelope from the mail box. The mail was just delivered. It was a letter from the University of Miami Medical School. The envelope contained information regarding donating body to medical science, and the forms to be signed by the donor. The family decided that it was too late because their aunt had died before signing the papers. They wished that the envelope had arrived a few days earlier. The nieces felt very guilty for not having contacted the University early in the year.

I perused the letter that was addressed to Jean, and gave it back to the nephew. We waited for the removal service to arrive to pick up the body.

Something prompted me to read that letter again. There were two lines at the bottom of that letter which said that the body could be donated after the death of the donor, if the next of kin signs a "declaration of consent." But that form was not included with the papers. Immediately I called the Remains Donation Department of the University of Miami whose number was listed at the bottom of the letter. A process was set in motion with signing and faxing of various documents which enabled the family to donate their aunt's body to medical science.

While all this was happening, the removal service called for directions, because they could not find the house. They apologized for being late. The irony is that the house was on a street that was easy to find, yet somehow they missed the street. If they had arrived on time, before the mail arrived, the body would have already been taken to the funeral home.

The niece said that usually the mail never arrives before four o'clock in that neighborhood. On this day, they had a mailman filling in for the regular one. The substitute mail delivery man decided to take a different route that day, and delivered the mail an hour early.

The series of happenings, such as the removal service being late, the mail being delivered earlier than usual, my impulse to take a second look at the letter—all worked together to make Jean's wish come true. The family members said that their aunt was a brave and generous woman who always helped others during her life. I pointed out to them the beauty of a life lived in generosity making the ultimate gift of life, even after death.

The family members of Jean shed tears of joy. My heart was filled with gratitude for the awesome blessing to participate in people's life journeys.

It is an amazingly humbling experience to be used as an instrument in the mysterious ways of the Spirit!

* * *

Ponder and Practice

> Do you have an experience similar to the one described in this story? Share it with a friend or group.

> Be open to the possibility that our loved ones may have the ability to influence events on earth after their death. No one *knows* enough about this realm to be pessimistic about it.

> Catholics pray *for* the souls of their loved ones, hoping to help them get out of purgatory. How about praying *to* our loved ones?

65. Bathroom Fall

Sid was 95. He was under hospice care, living in a nursing home in Florida. Although he had dementia, he was able to hold "real time" conversations, but did not have the ability to recall the past or imagine the future. Sid was a pleasant man, and I had a great time visiting with him.

After the visit, I called his daughter, Debra, who lived in New York. I started by saying that I had a beautiful visit with her wonderful father. "He may be wonderful to you, but not to me," she said. She added that her father was an alcoholic, and was abusive to her mother. Her mother committed suicide a week before Debra's wedding. Debra is still unmarried.

She had been estranged from her father for years, along with her brother who has had no contact with his dad for decades. Debra came into to the picture only recently because her father was admitted into hospice, and his end was near. "I am doing it only for ethical reasons; every minute I talk to you about my father is a minute wasted in my life," she said.

She advised me not to waste my time calling her in the future. Before ending our conversation, I told Debra that she may want to make peace with her dad as he was on hospice care. She said she would think about it.

Three weeks after my conversation with Debra, Sid died. The director of the nursing home could not get in touch with Debra, and so she texted a brief message: "Sid died at 8 a.m. this morning."

About 8.20 a.m. Debra came out of the bathroom, limping. She had fallen down in the bathroom, and had slightly strained her leg. She sat down on her bed and checked her phone. What shocked her was, not that her father had died, but that she fell down in the bathroom almost exactly the time he died.

What does that mean? Debra pondered!

As a hospice chaplain it is my job to call families of patients and offer them condolences. Based on my experience of the first call to Debra weeks before, I was a little nervous, but I called her anyway. I was pleasantly surprised by her response. I asked her if she had an opportunity to make peace with her dad, considering that she had untold animosity towards him. She had, in fact visited him once and made peace.

"Can I share with you something, chaplain?" she asked. I was all ears.

"This morning exactly at 8 a.m. when my father died, I fell down in my bathroom. I am a healthy woman. It has never happened to me before. I was shaving my legs as I have done a million times before, but today my knees buckled and I fell. I am okay; just a little bruised." "What do you think it means?"

I told her that I did not *know* what it means, but I know it means *something*.

She was open to the notion that her father may have been trying to tell her something.

I told her that after working in hospice for fifteen years, and having witnessed many deaths, I had re-defined death as "body leaving the soul" rather than "soul leaving the body."

"Your dad's soul, which is beyond all bodily limitations, is now able to *see* the big picture. When he met God, he might have asked for forgiveness for the folly of his ways during his earthly life. He is now able to *see* you for who you are—as his loving daughter, understand you fully, and love you unconditionally. By gently knocking you down, he now wants to lift you up to a new relationship with him."

"This is the most comforting conversation I had today," she said.

* * *

190

Ponder and Practice

> When someone dies, we usually say: "The soul left the body." What if we said: "The body left the soul"? What are the implications?

> Human beings are meaning-makers. Do you trust yourself enough to find your own meaning, or do you depend on others—teachers and preachers—to assign meaning to your experiences?

> "We come from *No-where*, we are *Now-here*, and we go *No-where*." What do you think about this statement from Wayne Dyer?

66. Two Flat Tires

Margie is 98 years old. When I walked into her apartment, she was sitting in her wheelchair and staring at the TV. She seemed weak, tired, and confused. Ninety-eight years of traveling on life's path seems to have weakened her lungs, blemished her skin in various spots, clouded her eyes, and the legs that carried her from Philadelphia to Phoenix, and then to Florida thirty years ago did not want to take another step. Margie had lived her life to the maximum and she didn't want to live any longer.

She asked me if I could do anything to hasten her exit from this world. "I have overstayed my welcome," she said. She was ready for the next stage of her journey. Her husband of 73 years sat beside her, holding her hand, and speaking words of love and reassurance to her.

Ron married Margie in the summer of 1942, immediately after the Second World War. Margie and Ron, are a rare breed these days—with a marriage that lasted over seven decades.

Ron who is also 98 years old, does not look his age. A retired dean of a business college, Ron is an intelligent man with a wide perspective on life. He is aware that nothing lasts forever and all good things must come to an end. He spoke lovingly about the wonderful life he and Margie had, the two boys they raised, and the three grandchildren they have. He teared up when talking about his son Paul, who died of a heart attack leaving two young daughters behind—ages two and five.

The topic of death is hard to broach, even in hospice setting. Therefore, I am reluctant to talk about it directly with caregivers, especially during the initial visit. However, having sensed Ron's breadth of awareness and realistic approach to life, I decided to bring up the topic. So I said: "Ron, you know Margie is going to pass on one of these days; it is going to be hard to continue this 73 year long journey alone."

"I could be gone, before she goes," he quipped.

"All things being equal, the likelihood of you surviving her is greater," I said.

"I am not going to be alone, because her spirit is going to be with me," said Ron. "I believe in after life," he added.

I was pleasantly surprised to hear that from Ron, being of the Jewish faith. Very rarely have I heard that statement from my Jewish patients or their caregivers. The conviction with which he made that statement, made me realize that he was not merely repeating a religious cliché about after-life.

"I am a true believer and I can tell you a true story to prove it," he said.

I had two sons, Rick and Paul. They were very close. Both got married, had successful jobs, and were settled in life. They used to visit as often as they could. At the end of every visit, Paul was reluctant to see his brother leave, and so he would jokingly threaten to let the air out of his tires so that he couldn't leave. The siblings loved each other so much.

In 1996, Paul, who was an avid runner, suddenly died of a heart attack, leaving his wife Lisa and two small children behind. It was a huge blow to our family.

A few days after Paul's death, Rick and his wife visited their grieving sister-in-law and the children. They spent a lot of time reminiscing about Paul. When Rick was getting ready to leave, Lisa jokingly said: "I am going to let the air out of your tires so that you can't leave." Those words brought tears of joy and sadness into everyone's eyes.

Rick and his wife hugged Lisa and the kids, promised to return sooner rather than later, and came out of the house to get into their car. They could not believe what they saw: The two front tires of their car were flat!

"That made a believer out of me," said Ron.

"Ever since that day, I have never doubted life after death. Yes, my wife's aging body is going to perish but her soul is going to live forever. That gives me comfort and hope."

* * *

Ponder and Practice

> When it comes to life after death, there are true believers like Ron and true skeptics. Where do you stand? Do you believe what you believe, based on your experience or because others told you so?

> When Ron says "her spirit is going to be with me" does he mean a "memory" or is it something "more"? Discuss the details of that "more."

>What do you think of the statement: "For something to be *real,* it doesn't have to be *physical.* In fact, sometimes *spiritual* realities can be more "real" than *material* realities. Think examples.

67. Heaven's Gate

Juan is 69 years old. His cancer had spread "all over the body" and his family was willing to let him go peacefully. They did not want him to live "with pipes and tubes" which he would have never wanted. His wife and three daughters made the hard decision to "pull the plug."

In hospice terms, it is called "extubation"—the process of removing the vents from a patient.

Extubation is often a heart-wrenching procedure accompanied by silent sobs of the loved ones standing around with tear-soaked faces. Juan's wife, three daughters, and two grandchildren had gathered around his bed in the ICU of a county hospital. I joined them in prayer and comforted them with words too imperfect to contain the pain of the moment or to express the emotions of the situation. Offering emotional and spiritual support to the anxious family members of an extubated patient can be exhausting.

While I was taking a breather outside the ICU, Juan's grandson, Phillip, walked up to me and asked: "Can I ask you a question?" I have always loved questions. In my view, there are no silly or stupid questions. So, I was glad that Phillip had a question. I had noticed that Phillip had a rosary around his neck, and looked like a very pious boy.

"Of course you can. What is it?"

"Do you think St. Peter will be waiting at the gate of heaven to receive grandpa?"

"Of course he will be," and I patted on Phillip's shoulder. He seemed relieved, wiped his tears, and went back into the ICU.

Phillip is an altar boy in his local parish. In his catechism class, he was taught that Catholics who die have three possible places to go: Heaven, Hell, or Purgatory. Heaven is reserved for those who live holy lives; very few if any, go there directly. You have to be a living saint, like Mother Teresa or a Pope, to deserve something like that immediately after death. Hell is for the unholy and it is permanent.

Purgatory is temporary and it is for those who need purification before the soul can move on to the next level—Heaven. Catholics believe that 99% of the souls go through purgatory before they get to Heaven.

Catholics are encouraged to pray for the souls in purgatory so that God can purify their souls and make them ready for heaven. These prayers are considered more needed especially during the days and weeks following the death of a loved one.

In the Catholic liturgical calendar, the month of November, which begins with "All Saints Day" and "All Souls Day," on the first and second day of the month respectively are set apart for special prayers for the souls in purgatory. Rituals include special prayers at the grave, and paying the priest to offer a "Mass for the repose of the soul" of the diseased. When I was young, I have paid priests to offer Mass for the souls of my grandparents. When I became a priest, I have offered Masses for the souls of many parishioners.

I have no idea how all that works.

I believe in heaven and hell. I am not sure about purgatory. I don't believe that heaven, hell or purgatory are physical locations, because a soul, by its very definition, is non-physical, and it doesn't need a place to reside. I don't believe that heaven and hell can be located on a Google map.

I gave Phillip an affirmative answer about St. Peter waiting for his grandpa, because a hospital ICU, right before the death of his grandfather, is not the right place or time for a theological discussion about after-life. I wish, however, that the Church stopped teaching children, the old catechism about pearly gates and singing angels.

I don't believe heaven is *a place*. I don't believe it is an exclusive gated community for the select few.

I don't believe it is about *going to a new location* as much as *experiencing the current location in a new way.*

I believe it is a *state of being* than a *place for beings.*

196

I believe heaven is all around me.

During my physical existence, I experience glimpses and slices of heaven, but when my bodily limitations end with death, I experience heaven all the time.

Heaven is about experiencing reality beyond the limitations of the five senses.

It is about seeing the big picture that was blocked from my view by the body.

It is about the dismantling of the ego and permanently wearing the mantle of the soul.

It is the immersion of my soul into the eternal Soul of God.

It is the merging of me—the small *i am* into the Big *I AM*.

Heaven is pure joy, perfect peace, and unconditional love—all at once!

* * *

Ponder and Practice

> Explain your notion/vision of heaven. Is it a repetition of others' teachings or an articulation of your own thoughts?

> If you are not in heaven *now,* you are unlikely to go there *later.* So the question is not *Do you want to go to heaven* but, *Is heaven in you?* "It's heaven all the way to heaven." ~Catherine of Siena

> Let's say everything ends this side of the grave, and there is no after-life in heaven, hell or purgatory. Will that prospect change your current life in any way?

68. I Could be Harry

Shirley is a patient on my hospice team who is 88 years old. She is diagnosed with heart disease, but prides in the fact that her head is still good. Shirley can engage in meaningful conversations, although sometimes she struggles to come up with the right words. She is always delighted to see me. The reason for that special delight is that I remind her of her dad. "You look like my dad," she said the first time I visited her.

Shirley was very close to her dad. "I was his one and only favorite daughter," she says with a huge smile. Shirley was a professional piano player. Her dad used to attend all the events where Shirley played, sat on the front row, and cheered her.

One day she asked me if I was married and I said yes. "Some nice lady has gotten you," she said with a sigh. (My wife may have a different take on it). Then she added: "If you weren't married, I'd go after you, but I know it is too late for me."

Early on, I realized that Shirley's "attraction" to me is a case of *transference*—a phenomenon characterized by unconscious redirection of feelings from one person to another. It is the redirection of feelings and desires, especially of those unconsciously retained from childhood toward a new person.

Transference was first described by Sigmund Freud who found its value for better understanding of his patients' feelings. Transference can be good in both therapeutic and non-therapeutic situations. It can occur in everyday life. When people meet a new person who reminds them of someone else, they unconsciously infer that the new person has traits similar to the person previously known.

In addition to transference, I wondered if there could be a case for re-incarnation in this situation. So I asked Shirley to describe her dad to me.

His name was Harry. He always had a smile. He loved his children. He had one brother and three sisters. He sold men's clothing. He was very religious. He was president of his local synagogue when Shirley was growing up.

I realized that I had similarities with Harry in that I too have one brother and three sisters. I love my children. I try always to have a smile always. I am religious and while Harry sold men's clothing, I chose the profession of a "man of the cloth."

While the similarities may end there, I could not help think about re-incarnation. The word "reincarnation" derives from Latin, literally meaning, "entering the flesh again."

It is the religious concept that after physical death, the soul or spirit can begin a new life in a new body. This doctrine is a central tenet of the Hindu religion.

As a native of India and an admirer of Hinduism, I have a special affinity to the concept of reincarnation as a possible state of being after death. It is a possible explanation for *déjà vu*—the phenomenon of having the strong sensation that an event or experience currently being experienced has already been experienced in the past. I have had several *déjà vu* experiences with people who remind me of siblings I have lost early on. My special attraction to them can be explained by the fact that I was related to them in a previous life.

Whether it is transference or re-incarnation, the fact of the matter is that Shirley finds my visits "something to look forward to in this place where everything is so predictable." For her, our time together is one of the "most joyful experience in this otherwise drab place."

I am grateful and humble when I end my visit with Shirley with an assurance to return in a month—a promise she extracts from me before I leave.

* * *

Ponder and Practice

> Transference can be positive or negative. Make a list of individuals with whom you have felt transference. Explore the feelings behind those leanings.

> If you were to re-incarnate, think of ten things you would do differently from your current life. If you were married, would you marry again or choose to be single? Would you marry the same person or would you choose a different partner?

>Take out your smart phone, go to *Wikipedia* and read the article on *Reincarnation,* and discuss it with a friend or in a group.

69. Sol. Dad. God

It was a bright Monday. About twenty five residents were sitting around, most of them in wheel chairs, enjoying soft music in the "memory care unit" of an assisted living facility. I was there to visit a new patient admitted to my hospice team. Since I didn't know who it was, I asked: "Who is Sol?" and a tiny man in a wheelchair raised his hand and said: "I am here."

He was one of the few residents who was awake and alert, and was delighted that somebody had come to see him. I pushed his wheelchair out of the lobby area, took him to a quiet room, and sat next to him.

My connection to Sol was almost instant—he reminded me so much of my dad who died 14 years ago. I loved my dad deeply, and visiting family in India after his death has not been the same. I miss him so much. I "talk" to him often, but I had never met anyone who so closely resembled and reminded me of my dad, until today.

Sol resembled my dad in size and shape but most importantly by his face, and in the way he talked. Short sentences, words without filters, mischievous grin, silly laughs. Sol's toothless lower gum made his speech perfectly resemble that of my dad who had lost his lower teeth towards the end of his life. Before I was able to say anything to him, Sol asked: "What are you selling?"

Me: "Nothing."

Sol: "Then why are you here?"

Me: "I am a chaplain."

Sol: "I don't need one." He knew who a chaplain was because he had served in the US Army during WWII and is a Purple Heart recipient.

Me: "Why not?"

Sol: "Because that is a lot of baloney."

Me: "Tell me more about it."

Sol: "It is a game of money; they don't work for nothing; everybody wants money."

Me: "I don't want money." (Not a true statement, but that is what I felt like saying then)

Sol: "I guarantee you, if they offer you money, you will take it; do you get paid for this?"

Me: "Yes, I do."

Sol: "If you did this without getting paid for it, I will respect you more."

Despite such a challenging and often uncomfortable dialogue, my fondness for Sol did not diminish. It was a pleasure listening to the way he spoke. He told me about how his parents, who were immigrants from Poland and Russia, struggled to make a living in the United States. Sol did not have a chance to go to college because his parents couldn't afford it. He was proud to mention that more patents were created by Jews, percentage-wise.

He was also aware of the terrorist attack in Brussels which he brought up to argue that there was no God, because if there was a God, how come He didn't prevent it?

I did not want to enter into a deep theological discussion with Sol, but simply asked him if he believed in God. He said: "Yes and No." And he added: "I don't know what to believe; I never met Him," to which I responded: "I have," and Sol had this quizzical look.

Sol: "Where do you see God?"

Me: "In you!"

Sol ignored my response with a dismissive hand wave, but I was not deterred.

I told him that I saw God in people because every human being is created in the image and likeness of God. There is a "spark of divinity" in every human being which some people manifest but most people don't. I told Sol that it was easy to see God in him because he was funny and cheerful.

I saw God that day in Sol—a person that God used to give me the blessing of remembering my beloved dad—his presence, his smile, his simplicity; gratitude for the simple, humble, generous spirit he was and everything he taught me, especially the deep lesson about God the Father.

The paddy fields in front of our house in India would become a mini ocean during the monsoon season. I had to cross the field to go to my elementary school, a mile away on the other side. We had no water transport, like a boat or a canoe. So my father would carry me on his shoulders and walk across the field with water hovering around his neck, and deposit me on the other shore, safe and dry.

When I returned from school, I would call him from the other side: "*Ichacha...Ichacha...*(Indian for daddy) and he would get into the water to come and get me. I felt totally safe sitting on his shoulders with my tiny legs wrapped around his neck, dangling and touching the water. The vast expanse of the water didn't scare me because I was sitting on my father's shoulders. Never for a moment did I ever think he would drop me, or I would drown. It was total child-like trust and perfect safety.

That was my earliest experience of God's love and providence which has remained with me always. Over the years, that divine template has been fortified and strengthened by the image of the Good Shepherd carrying a lamb on his shoulders—*even though I walk through the valley of the shadow of death, I fear no evil, for Thou art with me!*

I love my *Ichachan*...I miss him...and then there is Sol....wow!

Thank you Lord!

* * *

Ponder and Practice

> Think of your dad today whether he was a good dad or a bad father. Write a letter expressing all your feelings towards him.

> What is your image of God? Is *He* and old man with a white beard sitting on a throne beyond the clouds? Write down five sentences about God that is meaningful and experiential to *you.*

> Do you have a God-experience that is foundational to your life? How does that affect your life today? Articulate that in writing.

70. Will I See Him Again?

My bereavement support group session was coming to an end. Every participant in the group had lost a spouse. The depth of a spouse's grief is usually directly proportional to the strength of their love. And Suzy was no exception. She is 91 years old and currently resides in an assisted living facility. She was married to her husband Nathan for 62 years, until his death five years ago at the age of 88.

"I cannot wait to join him in heaven," Suzy said.

He was a wonderful man. He is the best husband any woman could hope for. He was devoted and dedicated. I was a war bride—WWII. He was the most wonderful man. He never stopped kissing me. He would come home from work and we were like newlyweds. His father used to say: "Aren't you ashamed to be like teenagers?"

Unfortunately, Nathan had Alzheimer's. I had to put him in a nursing home. It broke my heart. After each visit to the nursing home, I would come home with a broken heart, hysterically crying. He didn't know who I was and that killed me. I would hold him and hug him but he had no response to me. It was devastating...I think of him a thousand times a day. A minute doesn't go by without me thinking about him...I am waiting to join my loving Nathan.

"Chaplain Paul, let me ask you a question: "Will I see him again?"

Before giving my answer, I asked the group first. These were some of the responses:

"No; we are not going to see the dead ones again."

"I don't know."

"I don't think it is possible."

"I hope so." (Four of the participants had this response)

"I leave it up to God; He only knows."

Suzy was not the first person who ever asked that million dollar question—*Will I see my loved one again?* People in all cultures and religious traditions have been asking that question for generations. I don't think there is a definitive and final answer because, human life is like a book whose first and last chapters are missing. No one "knows" for sure where we *come from* before we took the physical form, and where we *go to* after we shed the physical form.

Humans in their search for security and certainty have come up with clichés and platitudes. I believe that every answer that we have come up with is speculation at best.

I am reminded of a story in the gospel of Mark (12: 18-26), where Jesus was asked about marriage in heaven.

Then the Sadducees, who say there is no resurrection, came to him with a question. 19 "Teacher," they said, "Moses wrote for us that if a man's brother dies and leaves a wife but no children, the man must marry the widow and have children for his brother. 20 Now there were seven brothers. The first one married and died without leaving any children. 21 The second one married the widow, but he also died, leaving no child. It was the same with the third. 22 In fact, none of the seven left any children. Last of all, the woman died too. 23 At the resurrection whose wife will she be, since all seven were married to her?" 24 Jesus replied, "Are you not in error because you do not know the Scriptures or the power of God? 25 When the dead rise, they will neither marry nor be given in marriage; they will be like the angels in heaven.

Like the Sadducees in this episode, Suzy is holding on to the hope of re-living her wonderful marriage again in a new realm. If that hope helps her cope today, more power to her. I don't have the information to tell her whether she is right or wrong in hoping for a reunion with her husband.

I don't spend a lot of time fantasizing about the future because every minute spent in speculating about the future is a minute less for living in the present. Therefore, I am not anxiously anticipating a reunion with loved ones or entirely discounting it as a possibility.

Based on my awareness about the nature of energy which cannot be destroyed but can only be transformed, I believe we will *see* our loved ones again.

Obviously I am not talking about "seeing" with our physical eyes because physical seeing is limited to this side of the grave. When our "eye-sight" disappears, "soul-sight" takes over. We don't have to wait until death to experience soul-sight. Soul-sight is possible for anyone who believes that our physical sight is imperfect, incomplete, and inadequate to encompass the enormity of reality.

Let me use an analogy to explain what soul-sight means in this context.

Imagine entering a room where fifty people are gathered. You scan their faces for thirty seconds, and realize that every one of them is a stranger except one person. That one person is your spouse. Now close your eyes. Forty nine faces have disappeared. One face remains in your consciousness, even though your eyes are now closed. You are still *seeing* your spouse—sensing her scent, hearing her voice. If you stand there for a few minutes with your eyes still closed, you can *see* your experiences with her, unspooling in your consciousness.

I think *seeing* your loved ones after death is something like that.

Suzy was intrigued by my "explanation" of a reality that defies explanation.

* * *

Ponder and Practice

> Engage in "soul-seeing" or "third-eye-seeing" and be comfortable with uncertainty, unpredictability, and unknowing.

> Focus on figuring out how to make *this life* better today rather than worrying about what happens in the *after-life!*

> "Some people claim there is no life after death," said a disciple.

"Do they?' said the Master noncommittally.

"Wouldn't it be awful to die—and never again see or hear or love or move?"

"You find that awful?" said the Master, "But that's how most people are even before they die." ~ Anthony De Mello

71. Tired of Living, Afraid of Dying

Dotty is 91 years old. She has been on my hospice team for two months. Most days, she sits in her wheelchair looking at the bare walls of her room. The television is always on, but the colorful pictures on the screen didn't seem to make any sense to her. She switched off the TV when I entered the room saying: "I keep it on for the noise; otherwise, it is dead quiet in here and I can't stand it."

Dotty is physically weak and mentally tired. She depends on her private aide for her basic physical needs. A steady supply of oxygen is delivered to her nostrils by two plastic tubes attached to a nearby oxygen tank which methodically hums in the corner of the room. "I am leashed to this damn machine; I can't go anywhere," she said.

Dotty emigrated from Austria to the United States in 1939 with her parents. She was 14 years old. Her family settled in Queens, New York, and 15 years later she got married, and raised a family of two children. She is happy about the life she has had.

"I got away from Hitler; I came here, I found a good man, and we had a good marriage; I have good children and great grandchildren. I can't complain about any of that. But, I am tired; this is no way to live; there is no quality to my life; I want to die. Can you help me?"

I asked her if she was ready to answer in the affirmative if God were to call her today, and she said: "I am tired of living but afraid of dying."

I felt that despite her desire to die, there was some tentativeness about what comes next. She was afraid of the unknown. Even though she said that she could go *up* or *down*, she was not sure about what that involved. Then she said: "I hope I go *up* because I haven't killed anybody; I haven't stolen from anybody; I have never been arrested for any wrong doing."

It was clear that Dotty's notions about heaven and hell as post death-destinations were mere religio-cultural clichés than deep spiritual convictions. She added: "When you die, you go six feet under and that is it; end of story; it is very nice to have the illusion of going to heaven; it makes you feel better, but my brain doesn't believe that."

When I asked her why she always pointed *up,* when talking about God and heaven, Dotty said: "I am not sure, it is just a habit, I guess." As far as Dotty is concerned, there is no life after death, because she doesn't *know* anything about it and nobody has ever come back to tell us about it.

I don't think that our lack of awareness about something proves the non-existence of the reality itself. For example, when we were in our mother's womb, we had no awareness of the life to come after our birth. We had no advance knowledge that we would be born into a world that has pizza and donuts and beaches, hills and valleys, cars, trains and planes, iPods, iPads and iPhones. We had no awareness that such a beautiful world existed, and yet it did.

Maybe there is a more beautiful and thrilling world awaiting us after we shed our temporal wrappings! No one *knows* enough to be a pessimist about it. When we were in our mother's womb, we lived in total darkness and mostly slept through the nine months. Is it possible, that despite being outside the womb, we continue to *live in the dark,* mostly *sleep-walking* through life, and that is why it is difficult for us to believe in life after death?

The bottom line is that death is the ultimate mystery and no one can *scientifically* prove or disprove *life* after death. We have the option to consider death as a *wall* or as a *door.* If you see death as a wall, everything ends when you take your last breath. If you see death as a door, something new begins at the end of your physical existence and it could be something unimaginably beautiful.

In my bereavement support sessions, I have met grieving spouses in both groups—the *wall group* and the *door group.* Those in the door group seem to cope with their loss much better than those in the wall group. They cope with their loss in a much more healthy fashion, and rarely sink into a state of *complicated grief*—intense grief that lasts beyond six months and interferes with daily functioning.

Those in the *door group* are more peaceful and optimistic about their lives and have a strong faith that they will be reunited with their loved ones again in some fashion, in some *place*.

Those in the *wall group* argue with the reality of impermanence, and they find it hard to accept loss as part of life. They usually hit their heads *against the wall,* and end up angry, bitter, and devoid of hope.

Personally, I find it easy to thrive in life by being part of the *door group.*

* * *

Ponder and Practice

> Why is it so difficult to dismantle the tribal and patriarchal notion of God as a Being who lives "Up there?"

> That notion is derived from the concept of a flat earth, three thousand years ago. It is impossible to reconcile a "flat-earth theology" with a "round-earth cosmology." That may be the reason why Dotty's belief in a God "up there" did not alleviate her fear of death or offer hope for an after-life.

> If you want to have a meaningful life, you must "consciously unlearn" what you have "unconsciously learned" as children, about God, religion, and life itself.

72. Confirmation #MT253146

One April Sunday morning, I received the following text message: *Mom, Sybil went to be with the Lord at 3.00 this morning. Appropriate that she waited for Sunday, knowing her.* That was the message from our church administrator, informing us of the passing of Sybil, an elder at our church, who never missed a worship service.

I texted my wife Judy who was in Orlando, traveling: *Sybil checked into heaven at 3 a.m. and her confirmation number is: MT2531-46.* I have never announced the death of anyone like that before, but I was inspired to do so in Sybil's case.

Sybil was 95 years old. No, let me rephrase that—her body was 95 years old. Her spirit was ageless. She defied her age through her daring demeanor, always challenging conventional notions about how a person in the tenth decade of her life should believe and behave.

In 2014, at the age of 93, she pushed the boundaries of her health by doing the 5K run for *Compassion International.* It was hard for us healthy folks to navigate the sandy terrains of Dania Beach. We worried about her health. We wondered about her audacity in completing a task lesser humans won't even attempt. People in her age range are usually confined to their wheelchairs in nursing homes. But she woke up that Saturday morning and went to Dania Beach to complete the 5K run. Of course she walked, and was the last to reach the finish line, but she was determined to accomplish what she had set out to do.

Sybil actively participated in the *Habitat for Humanity* projects sponsored by the church. The project leader would always assign her light duties, like picking up garbage or painting a wall. But Sybil was not happy with that. She once climbed the ladder to work on the roof of the new house they were building. She forbade the group members from telling her daughter June about it. Sybil always pushed the envelope to help, to serve, and to be of use till the very end.

In her faith life too, Sybil had a similar approach—to explore the edges of her faith rather than be satisfied with what she already knew and believed. She had a curious mind. She was not afraid to be exposed to new ideas and insisted on reading my book *T.H.R.I.V.E: Six Keys to a Fuller Life*. I told Sybil that she didn't need to read it as she already had a full life, and she said: "I want to make it fuller." She attended every study group and discussion forum at the church.

Sybil was serious about her faith life. Her daughter, June, related a story from Jamaica. It was young June's 11th birthday. She wanted to invite her friends and have a party. Sybil suggested that June should consider inviting the children from the "Home for the Handicapped" for the party, rather than her friends who were well off. June took her mother's advice and invited those children and had a great party. It was a life changing experience for young June.

Sybil who took the teachings of Jesus seriously, was encouraging her daughter to heed the advice of Jesus: "When you give a luncheon or a dinner, do not invite your friends or your brothers or your relatives or rich neighbors, otherwise they may also invite you in return and that will be your repayment. But when you give a reception, invite *the poor, the crippled, the lame, the blind,* and you will be blessed, since they do not have the means to repay you; for you will be repaid at the resurrection of the righteous." (Luke 14:12-14)

Sybil always cared deeply about the poor and the disadvantaged. She was an active volunteer at the *Gateway Program* at Royal Palm Christian Church, where food was distributed to the poor and the homeless on Thursdays. She was also involved in prison ministry. Sybil was active in all these ministries six months prior to her death. She seemed to understand the meaning of the story of the *Sheep and the Goats* in the gospel of Mathew and put it into practice.

I am convinced that on the Sunday morning of her death, Jesus greeted her with these words:

"Come, you who are blessed by my Father; take your inheritance, the kingdom prepared for you since the creation of the world. For I was hungry, and you gave me something to eat, I was thirsty, and you gave me something to drink, I was a stranger, and you invited me in. I needed clothes and you clothed me, I was sick, and you looked after me, I was in prison, and you came to visit me. (Mathew 25:34-36)

I have no doubt Sybil is in the Kingdom of Heaven and that is why I "received" the confirmation number MT25:31-46!

* * *

Ponder and Practice

> Imagine you are planning a party for you or your family—birthday, graduation, anniversary etc. The budget is $1000. Would you consider canceling the party and donating that money to a homeless shelter? How about donating $500? How about $100?

> Wouldn't it be great if you could make an advance reservation for heaven? It is possible! No credit card required. Have a compassionate heart for the least, the lost, and the last.

> Imagine living in a world where the divinity within you is always affirmed, and the divinity within others is never denied.

73. Tears and Laughter

A bereavement support group is a heavy place. Nobody goes there unless they have to, and the main purpose of attending such a group is to unburden oneself of the unbearable pain of losing a loved one. In such a group, sighs are audible, tears are visible, and emotions are palpable. Kleenex boxes are must-have-items for such groups where it will be liberally used.

The sessions lasted for 90 minutes. I made a decision to use the first 70 minutes to share feelings, the next 15 to explore coping strategies, and the last 5 minutes to intentionally laugh. I had great success with that format, and the participants seemed to be very pleased with the benefits of being part of such a group.

In every group there were one or two who felt uncomfortable with the idea of laughing in a grief support group. "I don't feel like laughing while I am grieving the loss of my husband," said one widow. I told her that laughter does not diminish or remove the pain of loss but it mitigates it, even for a moment. Besides, I believe that happiness and sadness are emotional siblings. That is why when we laugh out loud and cry our hearts out, tears come out.

The laughter segment of our support group was carefully planned. Participants were asked to bring a joke to share with the group.

Bob, who joined our group after the death of his wife, took his assignment seriously. I instantly liked Bob for his calm demeanor and devilish grin that was both charming and disarming. Bob really helped the group members by sharing insights and ideas, but he was more famous for the jokes he told at the end of each session.

Bob took his role as "resident joke teller" seriously. On the eve of the support group, he would do research on the internet to find a joke that was both funny and relevant. And he had a dry, flawless delivery that made the punch line even more pungent.

One day he brought an Indian joke to poke fun at me.

When a woman gets married in India, she brings a dowry into the union. On the wedding night, the groom scratches the dot on his bride's forehead to find out if he has won a convenience store, a gas station, a Dunkin Donuts shop, or a motel in the United states. If the dot reveals none of the above, he must stay in India and provide technical support to Americans!

Bob then added another line to make it applicable to me: *He must come to America to conduct grief support groups.*

A few months after leaving the support group, Bob died. I had the honor of doing Bob's funeral. His daughter said that her dad was a happy man, always joking and making others laugh. He was an organ donor. His children wondered what organ of an 81 year old man could be of any use to anyone. His son-in-law remarked: "His funny bones."

I could not end Bob's funeral service without telling a funny story. This is the story Bob told the group during the last meeting he attended.

A couple, desperate to conceive a child, went to their priest and asked him to pray for them. "I am going on a sabbatical to Rome, and while I am there, I'll light a few candles for you at St. Peter's Basilica, and pray for you," he offered.

When the priest returned few years later, he went to the couple's house and found the wife pregnant and busy attending to two sets of twins. He was elated his candles and prayers had worked. The priest asked the woman where her husband was so that he could congratulate him.

And the wife said: "He's gone to Rome to blow out the candles you lit."

Thank you Bob for making us laugh during many meetings.

* * *

Ponder and Practice

> A four year old child laughs 40 times a day, a forty year old adult laughs 4 times a day. What happened?

> "Laughter is the tonic, the relief and the surcease for your pain." "To truly laugh, you must be able to take your pain and play with it." "A day without laughter is a day wasted." ~ Charlie Chaplin

> Why did the students eat their homework? (because, the teacher told them it was *a piece of cake)*

74. Hospital Wedding

Hi, Reverend Paul, my name is Jon W. and I am at the Aventura Hospital. One of the nurses here gave me your card. I'm in dire need of your services. I am in room 620 of the step-down unit of the critical care. Please give me a call as soon as you get this message.

Not knowing who Jon was or what he was calling about, I returned his call. He said that he had come down with a serious case of sepsis, and was admitted to the hospital. He is not sure if he is going to get out alive this time. He was supposed to get married next week and the chances of that happening are remote. He requested that I do a marriage ceremony for him in his hospital room.

Jon is Catholic. He had made a couple of phone calls to the nearby churches but no priest would marry him in the hospital. They would only do the service in the church. Jon, a life-long Catholic, was disappointed.

At 7 o'clock on Wednesday, December 16, 2015, I walked into room 620 at Aventura hospital. John was in bed, hooked up to IVs. His fiancé Marcia, was sitting next to his bed. Instantly, I felt a connection to them. They were processing a plethora of undifferentiated emotions clogging their minds. A hospital room is not a place for a wedding. Jon knew that there was a remote possibility of him not getting out of the hospital alive. Marcia knew that there was a possibility of her walking out of that hospital as a widow, a few hours or days after she became a wife.

It was one of the saddest moments of my life. I thought of all the weddings I had officiated in the past, the latest being just four days earlier in a posh estate in Miami, for a young couple who were dancing with joy at the beach-side resort. They were surrounded by nearly 250 people, family and friends. The contrast between that beach wedding and this hospital wedding is incomparable.

Jon was 56, and Marcia was 59. They had no family to surround them. Their parents were divorced. They were estranged from their siblings. Jon and Marcia had known each other for ten years and their plan to get married in a private ceremony surrounded by a few friends had to be squashed.

Here I am sitting at the bedside of a critical patient who is the groom and his fiancé next to his bed, and my heart is filled with sadness and compassion. I prayed for the right words to speak to them and bring a sense of peace into a situation where nothing of that kind was easily available.

I spoke to them about grace surrounding them. I told them that God is with us even in the darkest moment of our lives. I congratulated them for the depth of love they were manifesting at this critical time.

Jon's desire to do right by his woman brought tears into Marcia's eyes. Marcia's devotion to Jon, and her desire to marry him at his hospital bedside, brought tears into his eyes.

At the end, with the shadow of death casting over them, I placed Jon's right hand in Marcia's and helped them say the vows. When Jon said, "I, Jon take you, Marcia, as my lawfully wedded wife," both burst into tears...it took a full minute to continue with the vows.

In regular weddings, the phrase, "until death do us part" is an inane line, unconsciously uttered by giddy couples. But tonight, that phrase seemed to be the most potent words of the moment and it was hard to hear them repeat it. It took me to a place of utter sadness and compassion for Jon and Marcia.

At the end of the ceremony, I reflected on the forces of the Universe that brought the three of us from totally different backgrounds and experiences to that particular moment in a hospital room in South Florida. I told them that it was a *Godincidence*, not a coincidence.

Jon was of Polish descent born and raised in Alabama. Marcia was of Italian descent born and raised in Miami. I am of Indian descent, born and raised in Kerala, India. In my 27 years of living in Florida, I have never been to Aventura hospital. On this particular day, I am there with two human beings during one of the critical moments of their lives to bear witness to a bitter-sweet moment in their lives.

The connecting link between the couple and me was another human being named Rose, who is a nurse at the hospital. I had no memory of meeting Rose. Apparently, she had met me at a conference two years earlier, and I had given her my business card. She kept that card, and when Jon was desperate to find a priest who was willing to officiate the wedding in a hospital room, Rose thought about me and gave him the card.

The likelihood of so many events happening randomly is unimaginable. It was a moment of divine serendipity. God used a priest from India, and a nurse from Haiti to bring a moment of grace to two souls from Poland and from Italy who live in Florida.

At the end of the ceremony I prayed for total healing for Jon. I prayed that he leaves the hospital healed and healthy. And I promised to celebrate their wedding in an Indian Restaurant where my wife and I would join them. Both Marcia and Jon loved Indian cuisine.

On Friday March 18, 2016, I received a text from Jon. He was out of the hospital, and he and Marcia were enjoying married life. I was delighted at the news. He wanted to celebrate the wedding at an Indian restaurant, as promised on the wedding day.

On March 20, 2016, my wife and I joined Jon and Marcia at the *Taste Buds of India* in Coral Springs, and celebrated their wedding with delicious Indian food and delightful conversations.

It felt like a foretaste of the feast in the *Heavenly Kingdom!*

* * *

Ponder and Practice

> At the end of each day, engage in an exercise called *examination of conscience* and review if any experience you had that day was a *Godincidence.*

> Stop labeling your experiences as *merely mundane.* Use your *soul-sight* to see every experience as a mystical dance choreographed by the master of the Universe.

> "You can live your life as if nothing is a miracle, or you can live your life as if everything is a miracle." ~ Albert Einstein

75. Young Old Man

Over the years, I have heard residents of assisted living facilities describing their homes as "hell holes," "nut houses," "insane asylums," and more. I have also heard the staff describing residents as "cranky old men," "bitches on wheels," or "zombies." So it was refreshing to meet a resident of an ALF who described the facility he lived in, as "paradise" and himself as the "luckiest man alive."

Ernie was 94 years old. He was the manager of a small factory in New York. His body was weak, but his mind was sharp, and he was a good story teller. When I visited, his aide was sitting next to him. Pointing to her, Ernie said: "When she walks in the door, I get energized; she is an amazing lady, my angel."

Ernie had recently moved into the ground floor apartment of that building. He was delighted that his room had a window and he could see outside. "Look at that window, now I can see the cars going by and people walking by; this is paradise," he said. He was so excited to show me a trophy he had won after getting a hole-in-one in a golf tournament in 2000. "I began playing golf from the moment I got out of my mother's womb (he laughs). It is so hard to get a hole-in-one. I am so happy."

Ernie knows what hospice care means. He is not afraid to talk about it.

"So, where do you go from here?" I asked, and he said:
"Turn around...you see that metal box?" He was pointing to the box that was sitting on his dresser with a crucifix on top of it. "That is the ashes of my wife...pick it up and see how heavy it

is...she was a large woman (he laughs)...I am going to join my wife...I had a wonderful life."

"So you have no fear of dying or regrets in life?"

"Of course not, none whatsoever, why should I? I had a great ride; I don't want to live ten more years like this; I was blessed to stay here this long watching my grandchildren grow up. The memories I gave them and the memories they gave me back are priceless; they have given me the best in my late years. Lord if you want me, take me."

Ernie talked enthusiastically about being able to attend the wedding of his only grandson two weeks earlier. He credited that achievement to St. Jude, his favorite saint. "I clutched the photo of St. Jude and prayed: you got to help me see Brian get married; and it happened. I'm so happy."

Noticing that I was writing notes, Ernie asked: "Are you going to write about me?" and I said: "As a matter of fact, I am writing a book, and I am going to include your story in it."

And he said: "It's going to be a best seller...but I don't want any royalty...even if you give it to me, I don't think I will be around long to collect it."

"From your lips to God's ears," I said.

"What title do you want me to use for your story?" I asked. Ernie thought for a moment and replied: *Young Old Man*. It is a perfect title for the story of a man who was unusually vibrant and vivacious for his age, especially mentally, and spiritually.

Ernie taught me that the phrase, "age is a matter of mind and if you don't mind, it doesn't matter" is not a cliché but a truth. He also taught me that *attitude matters*—in fact, that is all that matters, in life!

Unlike most people who look at a glass filled half-way with water and say: "It is half-full or half-empty," Ernie was doing something entirely different.

He doesn't waste his time "looking" at the glass or just sit back and opine about it. He takes hold of that glass, pours some whiskey into it, adds ice cubes, and say: "Cheers"!

Metaphorically, of course!

* * *

Ponder and Practice

> Ernie's effervescent personality consists of three basic ingredients: simplicity, humility and gratitude. How do you measure up?

> At the end of life, only two questions matter: 1) Were you a joyful person?, 2) Did you bring joy to others? If you want to increase your joy, copy and paste Ernie's ingredients to your life.

> Make it a habit to thank the person serving you in any venue using their names. Look at their name tags, use their name and say "Thank you ... " You will instantly create and experience joy.

Thank you...

A huge *Thank You* from the bottom of my heart to the hundreds of souls I encountered in the last fifteen years as a hospice chaplain—souls who inspired me, touched me, and taught me the life-changing lessons described in these stories.

Thank you my fellow-chaplains and friends—Kevin McGee, Larry Schuval, Grellet Sainvilus, Steven Jurgens-Ling, Tom Dalton, Jack Bloomfield, and Bill Kieffer for sharing your stories.

Thank you Misti for your inspiring leadership of the Vitas Broward chaplains, and for writing a generous foreword.

Thank you Mitch for your encouraging words and tips in the process of writing these stories, and for the awesome words on the back cover.

Thank you Judy, my wife, for editing the first draft, designing the cover, for continued moral support, and for offering critical comments and suggestions throughout the process of writing.

Thank you Piero Falci, my hero-friend, for so patiently formatting the interior text and for your valuable suggestions.

Thank you my friends, Bill Kieffer, Karen LeFever, and Nellie Bodrug for taking the time to edit these stories and offering valuable suggestions for improvement.

And *thank you* all the readers of these stories—may you be blessed and enriched by them as I am.

Made in United States
Troutdale, OR
09/22/2023